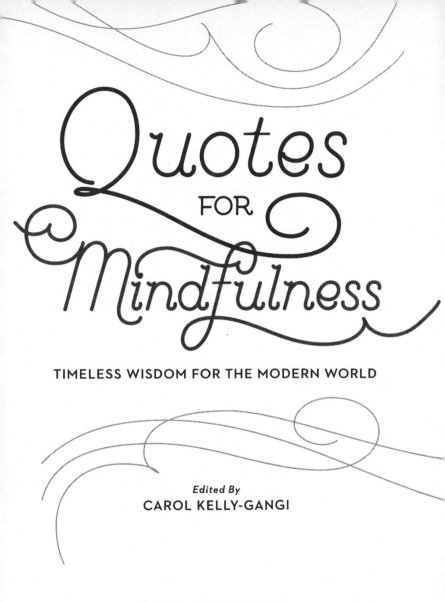

Quotes FOR Mindfulness

TIMELESS WISDOM FOR THE MODERN WORLD

Edited By
CAROL KELLY-GANGI

FALL RIVER PRESS

New York

FALL RIVER PRESS

New York

An Imprint of Sterling Publishing Co., Inc.
1166 Avenue of the Americas
New York, NY 10036

Fall River Press and the distinctive Fall River Press logo
are registered trademarks of Barnes & Noble, Inc.

ISBN 978-1-4351-6400-0

Distributed in Canada by Sterling Publishing Co., Inc.
$^{c}/_{o}$ Canadian Manda Group, 664 Annette Street
Toronto, Ontario, Canada M6S 2C8
Distributed in the United Kingdom by GMC Distribution Services
Castle Place, 166 High Street, Lewes, East Sussex, England BN7 1XU
Distributed in Australia by NewSouth Books
45 Beach Street, Coogee, NSW 2034, Australia

For information about custom editions, special sales, and premium
and corporate purchases, please contact Sterling Special Sales
at 800-805-5489 or specialsales@sterlingpublishing.com.

Manufactured in the United States of America

2 4 6 8 10 9 7 5 3 1

www.sterlingpublishing.com

Book design by Christine Heun

Contents

To my sisters,
Barbara, Theresa, and Marianne,
with love and gratitude

Introduction

Mindfulness has become a revolution. Millions of people around the world are devoting themselves to cultivating more mindfulness in their lives. Mindfulness programs are now offered in the workplace, in schools, in locker rooms, even in prisons. There are countless books, retreats, courses, apps, and websites guiding us toward mindful eating and parenting, offering mindful exercises to help combat anxiety and depression and to decrease our overall stress levels. In the insanely fast-paced world in which we are now living, it makes perfect sense that this ancient practice, rooted not only in Buddhism but also in all world religions, is providing a much-needed antidote to the stress and demands of life in our frenetic world.

What is mindfulness all about? As leading expert Jon Kabat-Zinn explains, "Mindfulness is awareness that arises through paying attention, on purpose, in the present moment, non-judgmentally." In *Quotes for Mindfulness,* we have gathered hundreds of quotations from speakers all over the world, all of which speak to some aspect of mindfulness. The selections are arranged thematically in categories such as Live Each Day; This Is the Moment; Free Your Mind; Find Your Inner Peace; Accept Change; Seek Simplicity; Love and Kindness; Joy and Happiness; Gratitude and Hope; and Compassion and Forgiveness.

And who are the men and women who share their wisdom on these fundamental themes? They are philosophers and scholars; artists and writers; monks and mystics; saints and sages; poets and politicians; religious leaders and world leaders; scientists and psychologists; and actors and activists, each offering insights that form a tapestry of ideas to help us grasp and implement mindfulness in our own lives.

Contributors such as Albert Einstein, Pope Francis, Henry David Thoreau, Lao Tzu, and Walt Whitman extol the value of simplicity. Deepak Chopra, Emily Dickinson, Goldie Hawn, Plutarch, and Eckhart Tolle each exhort us to live in the present moment. And Maya Angelou, the Dalai Lama, Mahatma Gandhi, Mother Teresa, and Thomas Merton reflect on the essential role of compassion and forgiveness. Revealing wisdom that is simple and profound, singular and universal, the contributors remind us to nurture the mind, body, and spirit; celebrate our common humanity; become our best selves; and witness the wonder and beauty all around us.

It is my great hope that the wisdom unearthed from this rich array of extraordinary men and women will inspire and challenge us to be ever mindful as we journey, moment by moment, through life.

—Carol Kelly-Gangi
2016

Mindfulness Is . . .

Mindfulness is awareness that arises through paying attention, on purpose, in the present moment, non-judgmentally.

—*Jon Kabat-Zinn*

Mindfulness is the aware, balanced acceptance of the present experience. It isn't more complicated than that. It is opening to or receiving the present moment, pleasant or unpleasant, just as it is, without either clinging to it or rejecting it.

—*Sylvia Boorstein*

Mindfulness in its most general sense is about waking up from a life on automatic, and being sensitive to novelty in our everyday experiences.

—*Daniel J. Siegel*

Mindfulness is simply being aware of what is happening right now without wishing it were different; enjoying the pleasant without holding on when it changes (which it will); being with the unpleasant without fearing it will always be this way (which it won't).

—James Baraz

•◆•

Mindfulness is often spoken of as the heart of Buddhist meditation. It's not about Buddhism, but about paying attention. That's what all meditation is, no matter what tradition or particular technique is used.

—Jon Kabat-Zinn

•◆•

To pay attention, this is our endless and proper work.

—Mary Oliver

•◆•

Mindfulness is a way of being present: paying attention to and accepting what is happening in our lives. It helps us to be aware of and step away from our automatic and habitual reactions to our everyday experiences.

—Elizabeth Thornton

•◆•

Mindfulness is a quality that's always there. It's an illusion that there's a meditation and post-meditation period, which I always find amusing, because you're either mindful or you're not.

—Richard Gere

Mindfulness is knowing what you are experiencing while you are experiencing it. It is moment-to-moment awareness, has the quality of being in the now, a sense of freedom, of perspective, of being connected, not judging.

—*Guy Armstrong*

• ◆ •

Mindfulness is the quality of fullness of attention, immediacy, non-distraction. In that sense, it is the key to life.

—*Sharon Salzberg*

• ◆ •

Life is a dance. Mindfulness is witnessing that dance.

—*Amit Ray*

• ◆ •

Direct experience in the present moment has been described as a fundamental part of Buddhist, Christian, Hindu, Islamic, Jewish and Taoist teaching.

—*Daniel J. Siegel*

• ◆ •

A mind which is not protected by mindfulness is as helpless as a blind man walking over uneven ground without a guide.

—*Buddha*

• ◆ •

There's an inherent trap in trying to become a mindful person. Any moment that you are acting mindlessly you fall into the category of deficiency. You are less than what you are trying to be and this leads to some form of suffering.

—*Elisha Goldstein*

"Mindfulness" refers to that move where you notice your mind wandered. With mindfulness you monitor whatever goes on within the mind. "Meditation" means the whole class of ways to train attention, mindfulness among them.

—Daniel Goleman

• ◆ •

To be mindful entails examining the path we are traveling and making choices that alleviate suffering and bring happiness to ourselves and those around us.

—Allan Lokos

• ◆ •

We must especially learn the art of directing mindfulness into the closed areas of our life.

—Jack Kornfield

• ◆ •

Mindfulness isn't difficult, we just need to remember to do it.

—Sharon Salzberg

• ◆ •

Mindfulness doesn't cure all, but it always cures. It corrects the mind's natural tendency toward dispersion, diffusion, and agitation, redeploying mental energy toward insight, clarity, and well-being.

—Thich Nhat Hanh

Live Each Day

Nothing is worth more than this day.

—Goethe

•◆•

Begin at once to live, and count each day as a separate life.

—Seneca

•◆•

Wake at dawn with a winged heart and give thanks for another day of loving.

—Kahlil Gibran

•◆•

There is no enlightenment outside daily life.

—Thich Nhat Hanh

In today's rush, we all think too much, seek too much, want too much and forget about the joy of just being.

—Eckhart Tolle

• ◆ •

A bird doesn't sing because it has an answer, it sings because it has a song.

—Chinese proverb

• ◆ •

Slow down. Calm down. Don't worry. Don't hurry. Trust the process.

—Alexandra Stoddard

• ◆ •

Every day we are engaged in a miracle which we don't even recognize: a blue sky, white clouds, green leaves, the black, curious eyes of a child—our own two eyes. All is a miracle.

—Thich Nhat Hanh

• ◆ •

The man is happiest who lives from day to day and asks no more, garnering the simple goodness of life.

—Euripides

• ◆ •

We spend precious hours fearing the inevitable. It would be wise to use that time adoring our families, cherishing our friends and living our lives.

—Maya Angelou

How we spend our days is of course how we spend our lives.

—*Annie Dillard*

•◆•

Your daily life is your temple and your religion. Whenever you enter into it take with you your all.

—*Kahlil Gibran*

•◆•

To do the useful thing, to say the courageous thing, to contemplate the beautiful thing: that is enough for one man's life.

—*T. S. Eliot*

•◆•

It's only when we truly know and understand that we have a limited time on earth—and that we have no way of knowing when our time is up—that we will begin to live each day to the fullest, as if it was the only one we had.

—*Elisabeth Kübler-Ross*

•◆•

You had better live your best and act your best and think your best today; for today is the sure preparation for tomorrow and all the other tomorrows that follow.

—*Harriet Martineau*

•◆•

If you are depressed you are living in the past. If you are anxious you are living in the future. If you are at peace you are living in the present.

—*Lao Tzu*

Don't let yesterday use up too much of today.

—Cherokee proverb

• ◆ •

If your daily life seems poor, do not blame it; blame yourself, tell yourself that you are not poet enough to call forth its riches.

—Rainer Maria Rilke

• ◆ •

So teach us to number our days, that we may apply our hearts unto wisdom.

—Psalms 90:12

• ◆ •

I think, what has this day brought me, and what have I given it?

—Henry Moore

• ◆ •

One of the illusions of life is that the present hour is not the critical, decisive hour. Write it on your heart that every day is the best day in the year.

—Ralph Waldo Emerson

• ◆ •

Waking up this morning, I smile. Twenty-four brand new hours are before me. I vow to live fully in each moment and to look at all beings with eyes of compassion.

—Thich Nhat Hanh

I postpone death by living, by suffering, by error, by risking, by giving, by loving.

—Anaïs Nin

Tomorrow doesn't matter for I have lived today.

—Horace

A day is a miniature eternity.

—Ralph Waldo Emerson

This Is the Moment

Life is now. There was never a time when your life was not now, nor will there ever be.

—*Eckhart Tolle*

•◆•

Be happy in the moment, that's enough. Each moment is all we need, not more.

—*Mother Teresa*

•◆•

Gladly accept the gifts of the present hour.

—*Horace*

•◆•

Rejoice in the things that are present; all else is beyond thee.

—*Montaigne*

Above all, we cannot afford not to live in the present. He is blessed over all mortals who loses no moment of the passing life in remembering the past.

—Henry David Thoreau

. ✦ .

No mind is much employed upon the present: recollection and anticipation fill up almost all our moments.

—Samuel Johnson

. ✦ .

With the past, I have nothing to do; nor with the future. I live now.

—Ralph Waldo Emerson

. ✦ .

The only use of knowledge of the past is to equip us for the present. No more deadly harm can be done to young minds than by depreciation of the present. The present contains all that there is. It is holy ground; for it is the past, and it is the future.

—Alfred North Whitehead

. ✦ .

The best thing about the future is that it comes only one day at a time.

—Abraham Lincoln

. ✦ .

I never think of the future. It comes soon enough.

—Albert Einstein

Real generosity toward the future lies in giving all to the present.

—*Albert Camus*

•◆•

Breathe. Let go. And remind yourself that this very moment is the only one you know you have for sure.

—*Oprah Winfrey*

•◆•

Drink your tea slowly and reverently, as if it is the axis on which the world earth revolves—slowly, evenly, without rushing toward the future; live the actual moment. Only this moment is life.

—*Thich Nhat Hanh*

•◆•

Living in the present moment creates the experience of eternity.

—*Deepak Chopra*

•◆•

The whole of life is but a moment of time. It is our duty, therefore, to use it, not to misuse it.

—*Plutarch*

•◆•

If you surrender completely to the moments as they pass, you live more richly those moments.

—*Anne Morrow Lindbergh*

I like to bury my face in the sunny smell of the sheet on the line before I take it down. I like the slow squeak of the line through the rusty pulley as I haul in another sweet pillowcase. The laundry lines of my childhood made exactly that noise.

—*Susan Moon*

• ◆ •

The older one gets, the more one feels that the present moment must be enjoyed, comparable to a state of grace.

—*Marie Curie*

• ◆ •

Act in the moment, live in the present, slowly don't allow the past to interfere, and you will be surprised that life is such an eternal wonder, such a mysterious phenomenon and such a great gift that one simply feels constantly in gratitude.

—*Osho*

• ◆ •

Why not just live in the moment, especially if it has a good beat?

—*Goldie Hawn*

• ◆ •

We inhabit ourselves without valuing ourselves, unable to see that here, now, this very moment is sacred; but once it's gone— its value is incontestable.

—*Joyce Carol Oates*

Every moment that I am centered in the future, I suffer a
temporary loss of this life.

—*Hugh Prather*

Forever—is composed of Nows—

—*Emily Dickinson*

People sacrifice the present for the future. But life is available
only in the present. That is why we should walk in such a way
that every step can bring us to the here and the now.

—*Thich Nhat Hanh*

I have realized that the past and future are real illusions, that
they exist in the present, which is what there is and all there is.

—*Alan Watts*

You must live in the present, launch yourself on every wave,
find your eternity in each moment.

—*Henry David Thoreau*

Free Your Mind

My apprehensions come in crowds;
I dread the rustling of the grass;
The very shadows of the clouds
Have power to shake me as they pass:
I question things and do not find
One that will answer to my mind;
And all the world appears unkind.

—William Wordsworth

• ◆ •

Do not encumber your mind with useless thoughts. What good does it do to brood on the past or anticipate the future? Remain in the simplicity of the present moment.

—Dilgo Khyentse Rinpoche

A man should remove not only unnecessary acts, but also unnecessary thoughts, for then superfluous activity will not follow.

—*Marcus Aurelius*

When the mind is full of memories and preoccupied by the future, it misses the freshness of the present moment. In this way, we fail to recognize the luminous simplicity of mind that is always present behind the veils of thought.

—*Matthieu Ricard*

Of course I realized there was a measure of danger. Obviously I faced the possibility of not returning when I first considered going. Once faced and settled there really wasn't any good reason to refer to it again.

—*Amelia Earhart*

If your eyes are blinded with your worries, you cannot see the beauty of the sunset.

—*Jiddu Krishnamurti*

The day is never so dark, nor the night even, but that the laws of light still prevail, and so may make it light in our minds if they are open to the truth. I never yet knew the sun to be knocked down and rolled through a mud puddle; he comes out honor-bright from behind every storm.

—*Henry David Thoreau*

If water derives lucidity from stillness, how much more the faculties of the mind!

—*Chuang Tzu*

How much pain they have cost us, the evils which have never happened.

—*Thomas Jefferson*

Tell your heart that the fear of suffering is worse than the suffering itself. And no heart has ever suffered when it goes in search of its dream.

—*Paulo Coelho*

Most people don't realize that the mind constantly chatters. And yet, that chatter winds up being the force that drives us much of the day in terms of what we do, what we react to, and how we feel.

—*Jon Kabat-Zinn*

One way to boost our will power and focus is to manage our distractions instead of letting them manage us.

—*Daniel Goleman*

The perplexity of life arises from there being too many interesting things in it for us to be interested properly in any of them.

—*G. K. Chesterton*

For him who has no concentration, there is no tranquility.

—*Bhagavad Gita*

•◆•

We should have much peace if we would not busy ourselves with the sayings and doings of others.

—*Thomas à Kempis*

•◆•

Don't believe everything you think. Thoughts are just that—thoughts.

—*Allan Lokos*

•◆•

The primary cause of unhappiness is never the situation but thought about it. Be aware of the thoughts you are thinking. Separate them from the situation, which is always neutral. It is as it is.

—*Eckhart Tolle*

•◆•

If you look into your own heart, and you find nothing wrong there, what is there to worry about? What is there to fear?

—*Confucius*

•◆•

A single gentle rain makes the grass many shades greener. So our prospects brighten on the influx of better thoughts.

—*Henry David Thoreau*

The greatest weapon against stress is our ability to choose one thought over another.

—*William James*

• ◆ •

Give not reins to your inflamed passions; take time and a little delay; impetuosity manages all things badly.

—*Publius Statius*

• ◆ •

Anger cannot be overcome by anger. If a person shows anger to you, and you show anger in return, the result is a disaster. In contrast, if you control your anger and show its opposite—love, compassion, tolerance, and patience—then not only will you remain in peace, but the anger of others also will gradually diminish.

—*Dalai Lama*

• ◆ •

I have learned through bitter experience the one supreme lesson to conserve my anger, and as heat conserved is transmitted into energy, even so our anger controlled can be transmitted into a power that can move the world.

—*Mahatma Gandhi*

• ◆ •

If you get angry easily, it may be because the seed of anger in you has been watered frequently over many years, and unfortunately you have allowed it or even encouraged it to be watered.

—*Thich Nhat Hanh*

For every minute you are angry, you lose sixty seconds of happiness.

—*Ralph Waldo Emerson*

•◆•

Conflict cannot survive without your participation.

—*Wayne Dyer*

•◆•

Worry does not empty tomorrow of its sorrow. It empties today of its strength.

—*Corrie ten Boom*

•◆•

Therefore do not worry about tomorrow, for tomorrow will worry about itself. Each day has enough troubles of its own.

—*Matthew 6:24*

•◆•

Happy is the man who has broken the chains which hurt the mind, and has given up worrying, once and for all.

—*Ovid*

•◆•

Do not anticipate trouble or worry about what may never happen. Keep in the sunlight.

—*Benjamin Franklin*

•◆•

Be patient toward all that is unsolved in your heart and try to love the questions themselves.

—*Rainer Maria Rilke*

Find Your Inner Peace

There is only one journey. Going inside yourself.

—Rainer Maria Rilke

• ◆ •

The mind is never right but when it is at peace within itself.

—Seneca

• ◆ •

Our soul makes constant noise, but it has a silent place we never hear.

—Simone Weil

• ◆ •

Your vision will become clear only when you look into your heart. Who looks outside, dreams. Who looks inside, awakens.

—Carl Jung

We need to be quiet. We need to be happy. We need to be still. God's holy peace is all around me. When I am still, it is reflected within me.

—*Hugh Prather*

·•·

Do not feel lonely, the entire universe is within you.

—*Rumi*

·•·

I have never found a companion that was so companionable as solitude.

—*Henry David Thoreau*

·•·

In solitude a dialogue always arises, because even in solitude there are always two.

—*Hannah Arendt*

·•·

Solitude is not something you must hope for in the future. Rather, it is a deepening of the present, and unless you look for it in the present you will never find it.

—*Thomas Merton*

·•·

Between stimulus and response there is a space, and in that space lies our power and our freedom.

—*Viktor E. Frankl*

Silence is the universal refuge, the sequel to all dull discourses and all foolish acts, a balm to our every chagrin, as welcome after satiety as after disappointment.

—*Henry David Thoreau*

Each of us needs periods in which our minds can focus inwardly. Solitude is an essential experience for the mind to organize its own processes and create an internal state of resonance. In such a state, the self is able to alter its constraints by directly reducing the input from interactions with others.

—*Daniel J. Siegel*

Learn to get in touch with the silence within yourself and know that everything in this life has a purpose.

—*Elisabeth Kübler-Ross*

There are voices which we hear in solitude, but they grow faint and inaudible as we enter into the world.

—*Ralph Waldo Emerson*

None but ourselves can free our minds.

—*Bob Marley*

We must be true inside, true to ourselves, before we can know a truth that is outside us.

—*Thomas Merton*

Peace of mind is that mental condition in which you have accepted the worst.

—*Lin Yutang*

• ◆ •

If there is to be any peace it will come through being, not having.

—*Henry Miller*

• ◆ •

With all the demands placed on our time and energy by the world around us, it might seem counterintuitive to think that seeking stillness, rather than picking up the pace, is the key to becoming better people, friends, citizens of the world, and business-people.

—*Russell Simmons*

• ◆ •

My life is better when I get still regularly. Call it meditation or call it quiet time—doesn't matter. The benefits are the same. If you stay with the practice, it's like developing spiritual muscle.

—*Oprah Winfrey*

• ◆ •

Even before smart phones and the Internet, we had many ways to distract ourselves. Now that's compounded by a factor of trillions.

—*Jon Kabat-Zinn*

Nothing is so intolerable to man as being fully at rest.

—Blaise Pascal

• ◆ •

You must learn to be still in the midst of activity and to be vibrantly alive in repose.

—Indira Gandhi

• ◆ •

Meditation is simply about being yourself and knowing about who that is. It is about coming to realize that you are on a path whether you like it or not, namely the path that is your life.

—Jon Kabat-Zinn

• ◆ •

Meditation is not a way of making your mind quiet. It's a way of entering into the quiet that's already there—buried under the 50,000 thoughts the average person thinks every day.

—Deepak Chopra

• ◆ •

Meditation brings wisdom; lack of meditation leaves ignorance. Know well what leads you forward and what holds you back, and choose the path that leads to wisdom.

—Buddha

• ◆ •

Meditation is not a means to an end. It is both the means and the end.

—Jiddu Krishnamurti

We are sick with fascination for the useful tools of names and numbers, of symbols, signs, conceptions and ideas. Meditation is therefore the art of suspending verbal and symbolic thinking for a time, somewhat as a courteous audience will stop talking when a concert is about to begin.

—*Alan Watts*

Meditation practice isn't about trying to throw ourselves away and become something better. It's about befriending who we are already.

—*Pema Chödrön*

Meditation is the ultimate mobile device; you can use it anywhere, anytime, unobtrusively.

—*Sharon Salzberg*

Inside myself is a place where I live all alone and that's where you renew your springs that never dry up.

—*Pearl S. Buck*

Imagine that your mind is like a calm, clear lake or a vast empty sky: Ripples appear on the surface of the lake and clouds pass across the sky, but they soon disappear without altering the natural stillness.

—*Kathleen McDonald*

Let your mind wander in the pure and simple. Be one with the infinite. Let all things take their course.

—*Chuang Tzu*

• ◆ •

To experience peace does not mean that your life is always blissful. It means that you are capable of tapping into a blissful state of mind amidst the normal chaos of a hectic life.

—*Jill Bolte Taylor*

• ◆ •

Mindfulness meditation doesn't change life. Life remains as fragile and unpredictable as ever. Meditation changes the heart's capacity to accept life as it is.

—*Sylvia Boorstein*

• ◆ •

Do you have the patience to wait till your mud settles and the water is clear? Can you remain unmoving till the right action arises by itself?

—*Lao Tzu*

• ◆ •

The solution to my life occurred to me one evening while I was ironing a shirt.

—*Alice Munro*

• ◆ •

The thoughts that come to us are worth more than the ones we seek.
—*Joseph Joubert*

There is no need to go to India or anywhere else to find peace.
You will find that deep place of silence right in your room, your
garden or even your bathtub.

—*Elisabeth Kübler-Ross*

• ◆ •

Peace is joy at rest and joy is peace on its feet.

—*Anne Lamott*

• ◆ •

The ordinary arts we practice every day at home are of more
importance to the soul than their simplicity might suggest.

—*St. Thomas More*

• ◆ •

Do not lose your inward peace for anything whatsoever, even if
your whole world seems upset.

—*St. Francis de Sales*

• ◆ •

Feelings come and go like clouds in a windy sky.
Conscious breathing is my anchor.

—*Thich Nhat Hanh*

Nourish Your Mind,
Body, and Spirit

Nourishing yourself in a way that helps you blossom in the
direction you want to go is attainable, and you are worth
the effort.

—Deborah Day

•◆•

Nurturing yourself is not selfish—it's essential to your survival
and your well-being.

—Renee Peterson Trudeau

•◆•

To keep a lamp burning we have to keep putting oil in it.

—Mother Teresa

Untilled ground, however rich, will bring forth thistles and thorns; so also the mind of man.

—*St. Thérèse of Lisieux*

• ◆ •

A house is no home unless it contains food and fire for the mind as well as for the body.

—*Margaret Fuller*

• ◆ •

There is no end to education. It is not that you read a book, pass an examination, and finish with education. The whole of life, from the moment you are born to the moment you die, is a process of learning.

—*Jiddu Krishnamurti*

• ◆ •

I have learned silence from the talkative, tolerance from the intolerant, and kindness from the unkind. I should not be ungrateful to these teachers.

—*Kahlil Gibran*

• ◆ •

When we are mindful, deeply in touch with the present moment, our understanding of what is going on deepens, and we begin to be filled with acceptance, joy, peace and love.

—*Thich Nhat Hanh*

Anything less than a contemplative perspective on life is an almost certain program for unhappiness.

—Father Thomas Keating

. ◆ .

To keep the body in good health is a duty, otherwise we shall not be able to keep our mind strong and clear.

—Buddha

. ◆ .

The body is a sacred garment. It's your first and last garment; it is what you enter life in and what you depart life with, and it should be treated with honor.

—Martha Graham

. ◆ .

If we are creating ourselves all the time, then it is never too late to begin creating the bodies we want instead of the ones we mistakenly assume we are stuck with.

—Deepak Chopra

. ◆ .

Whatever good results I find in my reflections come to me when I am walking.

—Goethe

. ◆ .

A vigorous five-mile walk will do more good for an unhappy but otherwise healthy adult than all the medicine and psychology in the world.

—Paul Dudley White

Health is no longer defined as just the absence of disease, but it is a joyfulness that should be inside of us at all times—it is a state of positive well-being which is not just physical, but also psychological, emotional and spiritual.

—*Deepak Chopra*

•-◆-•

We need to do a better job of putting ourselves higher on our own "to do" list.

—*Michelle Obama*

•-◆-•

Realize that this very body, with its aches and it pleasures . . . is exactly what we need to be fully human, fully awake, fully alive.

—*Pema Chödrön*

•-◆-•

There is more wisdom in your body than in your deepest philosophies.

—*Friedrich Nietzche*

•-◆-•

If anything is sacred, the human body is sacred.

—*Walt Whitman*

•-◆-•

Bodily vigor is good, and vigor of intellect is even better, but far above is character.

—*Theodore Roosevelt*

Dreams nourish the soul just as food nourishes the body.
The pleasure of the search and of adventure feed our dreams.

—Paulo Coelho

• ◆ •

The soul is the user, the body for use; hence the one is master,
the other servant.

—St. Ambrose

• ◆ •

The secret of health for both mind and body is not to mourn
for the past, not to worry about the future, nor to anticipate
troubles, but to live the present moment wisely and earnestly.

—Buddha

• ◆ •

When you discover something that nourishes your soul and
brings joy, care enough to make room for it in your life.

—Jean Shinoda Bolen

Accept Change

Nothing endures but change.

—Heraclitus

•◆•

All is change; all yields its place and goes.

—Euripides

•◆•

Change is the process by which the future invades our lives.

—Alvin Toffler

•◆•

We change, whether we like it or not.

—Ralph Waldo Emerson

It's not the strongest of the species that survive, nor the most intelligent, but the one most responsive to change.

—*Charles Darwin*

•─•─•

Just when I think I have learned the way to live, life changes.

—*Hugh Prather*

•─•─•

For a seed to achieve its greatest expression, it must come completely undone. The shell cracks, its insides come out and everything changes. To someone who doesn't understand growth, it would look like complete destruction.

—*Marcel Proust*

•─•─•

And the day came when the risk to remain tight in a bud was more painful than the risk it took to blossom.

—*Anaïs Nin*

•─•─•

If we don't change, we don't grow. If we don't grow, we are not really living.

—*Gail Sheehy*

•─•─•

We must always change, renew, rejuvenate ourselves; otherwise, we harden.

—*Goethe*

The human species is forever in a state of change, forever becoming.

—*Simone de Beauvoir*

Awareness is the greatest agent for change.

—*Eckhart Tolle*

All changes, even the most longed for, have their melancholy; for what we leave behind us is a part of ourselves; we must die to one life before we can enter another!

—*Anatole France*

Every human has the freedom to change at any instant.

—*Viktor E. Frankl*

Step out of the history that is holding you back. Step into the new story you are willing to create.

—*Oprah Winfrey*

When you're finished changing, you're finished.

—*Benjamin Franklin*

One must never lose time in vainly regretting the past or in complaining against the changes which cause us discomfort, for change is the essence of life.

—Anatole France

One must never lose time in vainly regretting the past or in complaining against the changes which cause us discomfort, for change is the essence of life.

Any real change implies the breakup of the world as one has always known it, the loss of all that gave one an identity, the end of safety.

—James Baldwin

If you don't like something, change it. If you can't change it, change your attitude.

—Maya Angelou

You cannot, you cannot use someone else's fire. You can only use your own. And in order to do that, you must first be willing to believe that you have it.

—Audre Lorde

If you don't like the road you're walking, start paving another one.

—Dolly Parton

Change your life today. Don't gamble on the future, act now, without delay.

—Simone de Beauvoir

There is a certain relief in change, even though it be from bad to worse; as I have found in traveling in a stage coach, that it is often a comfort to shift one's position and be bruised in a new place.

—*Washington Irving*

Have no fear of change as such and, on the other hand, no liking for it merely for its own sake.

—*Robert Moses*

The first resistance to social change is to say it's not necessary.

—*Gloria Steinem*

We must adjust to changing times and still hold to unchanging principles.

—*Jimmy Carter*

Lasting change is a series of compromises. And compromise is all right, as long your values don't change.

—*Jane Goodall*

Change will not come if we wait for some other person or some other time. We are the ones we've been waiting for. We are the change that we seek.

—*Barack Obama*

Today is not yesterday. We ourselves change. How then, can our works and thoughts, if they are always to be the fittest, continue always the same? Change, indeed, is painful, yet ever needful; and if memory has its force and worth, so also has hope.

—*Thomas Carlyle*

•◆•

We must be the change we wish to see in the world.

—*Mahatma Gandhi*

Seek Simplicity

Simple in actions and in thoughts, you return to the source of being.

—*Lao Tzu*

•◆•

Eat when you're hungry. Drink when you're thirsty. Sleep when you're tired.

—*Buddhist proverb*

•◆•

Bringing simplicity into our lives requires that we discover the ways in which our consumption either supports or entangles our existence.

—*Duane Elgin*

Our life is frittered away by detail . . . Simplicity, simplicity, simplicity. I say, let your affairs be as two or three, and not a hundred or a thousand; instead of a million count half a dozen, and keep your accounts on your thumbnail.

—Henry David Thoreau

• ◆ •

How many things are there which I do not want.

—Socrates

• ◆ •

Have nothing in your house that you do not know to be useful, or believe to be beautiful.

—William Morris

• ◆ •

Possessions, outward success, publicity, luxury . . . to me these have always been contemptible. I believe that a simple and unassuming manner of life is best for everyone, best for both the body and the mind.

—Albert Einstein

• ◆ •

As you simplify your life, the laws of the universe will be simpler; solitude will not be solitude, poverty will not be poverty, nor weakness weakness.

—Henry David Thoreau

• ◆ •

How many things can I do without?

—Socrates

Simplicity is the most difficult thing to secure in this world;
it is the last limit of experience and the last effort of genius.

—George Sand

Reduce the complexity of life by eliminating the needless wants
of life, and the labors of life reduce themselves.

—Edwin Way Teale

Besides the noble art of getting things done, there is the noble
art of leaving things undone. The wisdom of life consists in the
elimination of nonessentials.

—Lin Yutang

Simplicity is making the journey of this life with just baggage
enough.

—Charles Dudley Warner

Beware the barrenness of a busy life.

—Socrates

The art of art, the glory of expression and the sunshine of the
light of letters, is simplicity.

—Walt Whitman

Simplicity is the final achievement. After one has played a vast quantity of notes and more notes, it is simplicity that emerges as the crowning reward of art.

—Frederic Chopin

•◆•

A visible simplicity of life,
Embracing unpretentious ways,
And small self-interest
And poverty of coveting.

—Lao Tzu

•◆•

One always begins with the simple, then comes the complex, and by superior enlightenment one often reverts in the end to the simple. Such is the course of human intelligence.

—Voltaire

•◆•

The ability to simplify means to eliminate the unnecessary so that the necessary may speak.

—Hans Hofmann

•◆•

Live simply so that others may simply live.

—Mahatma Gandhi

•◆•

In everything, love simplicity.

—St. Francis de Sales

A simple lifestyle is good for us, helping us to better share with those in need.

—*Pope Francis*

Voluntary simplicity means going fewer places in one day rather than more, seeing less so I can see more, doing less so I can do more, acquiring less so I can have more.

—*Jon Kabat-Zinn*

I am convinced, both by faith and experience, that to maintain one's self on this earth is not a hardship but a pastime, if we will live simply and wisely.

—*Henry David Thoreau*

Love and Kindness

Love is the center of human life.

—Dalai Lama

Love is a fruit, in season at all times and within the reach of
every hand. Anyone may gather it and no limit is set. Everyone
can reach this love through meditation, the spirit of prayer, and
sacrifice.

—Mother Teresa

Falling in love you remain a child; rising in love you mature.
By and by love becomes not a relationship, it becomes a state of
your being. Not that you are in love—now you are love.

—Osho

Being deeply loved by someone gives you strength, while loving
someone deeply gives you courage.

—Lao Tzu

The supreme happiness of life is the conviction of being loved for
yourself, or, more correctly speaking, loved in spite of yourself.

—Victor Hugo

True love is both loving and letting oneself be loved. It is harder
to let ourselves be loved than it is to love.

—Pope Francis

Love is of all passions the strongest, for it attacks simultaneously
the head, the heart, and the senses.

—Lao Tzu

Love is when each person is more concerned for the other than
for one's self.

—David Frost

If you love a flower, don't pick it up. Because if you pick it up
it dies and it ceases to be what you love. So if you love a flower,
let it be. Love is not about possession. Love is about appreciation.

—*Osho*

• ◆ •

What we have once enjoyed we can never lose. All that we love
deeply becomes a part of us.

—*Helen Keller*

• ◆ •

Each time you love, love as deeply as if it were forever.

—*Audre Lorde*

• ◆ •

We are shaped and fashioned by what we love.

—*Goethe*

• ◆ •

Real love doesn't die. It's the physical body that dies. Genuine,
authentic love has no expectations whatsoever; it doesn't even
need the physical presence of a person. . . . Even when he is dead
and buried that part of you that loves the person will always live.

—*Elisabeth Kübler-Ross*

• ◆ •

Love is how you stay alive, even after you are gone.

—*Mitch Albom*

The heart of another is a dark forest, always, no matter how close it has been to one's own.

—*Willa Cather*

•◆•

You cannot save people. You can only love them.

—*Anaïs Nin*

•◆•

We have all known the long loneliness and we have learned that the only solution is love.

—*Dorothy Day*

•◆•

True love is but a humble, low born thing.
And hath its food served up in earthenware;
It is a thing to walk with, hand in hand,
Through the every-dayness of this workday world.

—*James Russell Lowell*

•◆•

For one human being to love another human being: that is perhaps the most difficult task that has been entrusted to us, the ultimate task, the final test and proof, the work for which all other work is merely preparation.

—*Rainer Maria Rilke*

•◆•

Perfect love means putting up with people's shortcomings, feeling no surprise at their weaknesses, finding encouragement even in the slightest evidence of good qualities in them.

—*St. Thérèse of Lisieux*

My feelings of love may be unbounded, but my capacity to be
loving is limited. I therefore must choose the person on whom
to focus my capacity to love, toward whom to direct my will to
love. True love is not a feeling by which we are overwhelmed.
It is a committed, thoughtful decision.

—*M. Scott Peck*

The love of our neighbor in all its fullness simply means being
able to say to him, "What are you going through?"

—*Simone Weil*

Every act of love is a work of peace, no matter how small.

—*Mother Teresa*

The worst sin towards our fellow creatures is not to hate them,
but to be indifferent to them; that's the essence of inhumanity.

—*George Bernard Shaw*

I have decided to stick with love. Hate is too great a burden to bear.

—*Martin Luther King Jr.*

Here is the rule: Love, and do what you will.

—*St. Augustine*

Whoever has loved knows all that life contains of sorrow and of joy.

—*George Sand*

If you're going to care about the fall of the sparrow you can't pick and choose who's going to be the sparrow. It's everybody.

—Madeleine L'Engle

Spread love everywhere you go. Let no one ever come to you without leaving happier.

—Mother Teresa

Love is the missing factor; there is a lack of affection, of warmth in relationship; and because we lack that love, that tenderness, that generosity, that mercy in relationship, we escape into mass action, which produces further confusion, further misery.

—Jiddu Krishnamurti

Hurt people hurt people. That's how pain patterns gets passed on, generation after generation. Break the chain today. Meet anger with sympathy, contempt with passion, cruelty with kindness. Greet grimaces with smiles. Forgive and forget about finding fault. Love is the weapon of the future.

—Yehuda Berg

Whenever we encounter another person in love, we learn something new about God.

—Pope Francis

The little unremembered acts of kindness and love are the best parts of a person's life.

—William Wordsworth

. ◆ .

Kindness in words creates confidence.
Kindness in thinking creates profoundness.
Kindness in giving creates love.

—Lao Tzu

. ◆ .

Be kind whenever possible. It is always possible.

—Dalai Lama

. ◆ .

What do we live for, if it is not to make life less difficult for each other?

—George Eliot

. ◆ .

One kind word can warm three winter months.

—Japanese proverb

. ◆ .

Wherever there is a human being, there is an opportunity for a kindness.

—Seneca

. ◆ .

When I was young, I used to admire intelligent people; as I grow older, I admire kind people.

—Rabbi Abraham Joshua Heschel

It is a little embarrassing that, after 45 years of research and study, the best advice I can give to people is to be a little kinder to each other.

—*Aldous Huxley*

* ◆ *

Right from the moment of our birth, we are under the care and kindness of our parents and then later on in our life when we are oppressed by sickness and become old, we are again dependent on the kindness of others. Since at the beginning and end of our lives we are so dependent on others' kindness, how can it be that in the middle we neglect kindness toward others?

—*Dalai Lama*

* ◆ *

What we do for ourselves dies with us. What we do for others and the world remains and is immortal.

—*Albert Pike*

* ◆ *

How far you go in life depends on your being tender with the young, compassionate with the aged, sympathetic with the striving and tolerant of the weak and strong. Because someday in your life you will have been all of these.

—*George Washington Carver*

* ◆ *

There is a ripple effect in helping another.

—*Kathleen A. Brehony*

Kindness gives birth to kindness.

—Sophocles

. ◆ .

All acts of service are meaningless unless they are given with love.

—Sai Baba

. ◆ .

And I am convinced now that each occasion for giving in charity strengthens the habit and makes it easier.

—William James

. ◆ .

I ask you one thing: do not tire of giving, but do not give your leftovers. Give until it hurts, until you feel the pain.

—Mother Teresa

. ◆ .

Darkness cannot drive out darkness; only light can do that. Hate cannot drive out hate; only love can do that.

—Martin Luther King Jr.

. ◆ .

Love and compassion are necessities, not luxuries. Without them, humanity cannot survive.

—Dalai Lama

. ◆ .

I shall pass through this world but once. Any good therefore that I can do or any kindness that I can show to any human being, let me do it now. Let me not defer or neglect it, for I shall not pass this way again.

—Mahatma Gandhi

Compassion and Forgiveness

The whole idea of compassion is based on a keen awareness of the interdependence of all these living beings, which are all part of one another, and all involved in one another.

—*Thomas Merton*

• ◆ •

True compassion means not only feeling another's pain but also being moved to help relieve it.

—*Daniel Goleman*

• ◆ •

Compassionate people are geniuses in the art of living, more necessary to the dignity, security, and joy of humanity than the discoverers of knowledge.

—*Albert Einstein*

Let us not underestimate how hard it is to be compassionate.
Compassion is hard because it requires the inner disposition
to go with others to places where they are weak, vulnerable,
lonely, and broken. But this is not our spontaneous response to
suffering. What we desire most is to do away with suffering by
fleeing from it or finding a quick cure for it.

—*Henri Nouwen*

A person who practices compassion and forgiveness has great
inner strength, whereas aggression is usually a sign of weakness.

—*Dalai Lama*

Until he extends his circle of compassion to include all living
things, man will not himself find peace.

—*Albert Schweitzer*

Compassion for others begins with kindness to ourselves.

—*Pema Chödrön*

I learned compassion from being discriminated against. Everything
bad that's ever happened to me has taught me compassion.

—*Ellen DeGeneres*

To love means loving the unlovable. To forgive means pardoning
the unpardonable. Faith means believing the unbelievable. Hope
means hoping when everything seems hopeless.

—*G. K. Chesterton*

Any ordinary favor we do for someone or any compassionate reaching out may seem to be going nowhere at first, but may be planting a seed we can't see right now. Sometimes we need to just do the best we can and then trust in an unfolding we can't design or ordain.

—*Sharon Salzberg*

The weak can never forgive. Forgiveness is the attribute of the strong.

—*Mahatma Gandhi*

When you are offended at any man's fault, turn to yourself and study your own failings. Then you will forget your anger.

—*Epictetus*

True reconciliation does not consist in merely forgetting the past.

—*Nelson Mandela*

To forgive is the highest, most beautiful form of love. In return, you will receive untold peace and happiness.

—*Robert Muller*

To err is human, to forgive divine.

—*Alexander Pope*

Forgive and ask to be forgiven; excuse rather than accuse.

—*Mother Teresa*

• ◆ •

I learned a long time ago that some people would rather die than forgive. It's a strange truth, but forgiveness is a painful and difficult process. It's not something that happens overnight. It's an evolution of the heart.

—*Sue Monk Kidd*

• ◆ •

When a deep injury is done us, we never recover until we forgive.

—*Alan Paton*

• ◆ •

As I walked out the door toward the gate that would lead to my freedom, I knew if I didn't leave my bitterness and hatred behind, I'd still be in prison.

—*Nelson Mandela*

• ◆ •

It's one of the greatest gifts you can give yourself, to forgive. Forgive everybody.

—*Maya Angelou*

• ◆ •

Self-compassion is simply giving the same kindness to ourselves that we would give to others.

—*Christopher Germer*

If your compassion does not include yourself, it is incomplete.
—*Jack Kornfield*

• ◆ •

Your problem is you're too busy holding onto your unworthiness.
—*Ram Dass*

• ◆ •

Nothing I accept about myself can be used against me to
diminish me.

—*Audre Lorde*

• ◆ •

A moment of self-compassion can change your entire day.
A string of such moments can change the course of your life.
—*Christopher Germer*

• ◆ •

Compulsive concern with "I, me, and mine" isn't the same as
loving ourselves. . . . Loving ourselves points us to capacities
of resilience, compassion, and understanding that are simply
part of being alive.

—*Sharon Salzberg*

• ◆ •

Only by learning to live in harmony with your contradictions
can you keep it all afloat.

—*Audre Lorde*

Forgive yourself before you die. Then forgive others.

—*Mitch Albom*

Sincere forgiveness isn't colored with expectations that the other person apologize or change. Don't worry whether or not they finally understand you. Love them and release them. Life feeds back truth to people in its own way and time.

—*Sara Paddison*

The practice of forgiveness is our most important contribution to the healing of the world.

—*Marianne Williamson*

Joy and Happiness

I find ecstasy in living; the mere sense of living is joy enough.

—*Emily Dickinson*

·◆·

If you are joyful, it will shine in your eyes and in your look, in your conversation and in your countenance. You will not be able to hide it because joy overflows.

—*Mother Teresa*

·◆·

Do anything, but let it produce joy.

—*Walt Whitman*

Grief can take care of itself, but to get the full value of joy you must have somebody to divide it with.

—*Mark Twain*

Joy is very infectious. We will never know just how much good a simple smile can do. Be faithful in little things. Smile at one another. We must live beautifully.

—*Mother Teresa*

Joy is being willing for things to be as they are.

—*Charlotte Joko Beck*

There is a very simple secret to being happy. Just cease your demand on this moment.

—*Buddha*

Happiness is a state of mind. With physical comforts if your mind is still in a state of confusion and agitation, it is not happiness. Happiness means calmness of mind.

—*Dalai Lama*

The basic root of happiness lies in our minds; outer circumstances are nothing more than adverse or favourable.

—*Matthieu Ricard*

But I don't think of the future, or the past, I feast on the moment. This is the secret of happiness, but only reached now in middle age.

—*Virginia Woolf*

. ◆ .

It is the very pursuit of happiness that thwarts happiness.

—*Viktor E. Frankl*

. ◆ .

Why not seize the pleasure at once? How often is happiness destroyed by preparation, foolish preparation!

—*Jane Austen*

. ◆ .

Happiness is produced not so much by great pieces of good fortune that seldom happen, as by little advantages that occur every day.

—*Benjamin Franklin*

. ◆ .

Our greatest happiness does not depend on the condition of life in which chance has placed us, but is always the result of a good conscience, good health, occupation, and freedom in all just pursuits.

—*Thomas Jefferson*

. ◆ .

Happiness is neither virtue nor pleasure nor this thing nor that but simply growth. We are happy when we are growing.

—*William Butler Yeats*

You will never be happy if you continue to search for what happiness consists of. You will never live if you are looking for the meaning of life.

—*Albert Camus*

• ◆ •

The meaning of life is just to be alive. It is so plain and so obvious and so simple. And yet, everybody rushes around in a great panic as if it were necessary to achieve something beyond themselves.

—*Alan Watts*

• ◆ •

The summit of happiness is reached when a person is ready to be what he is.

—*Erasmus*

• ◆ •

Yes, there is a Nirvanah: it is in leading your sheep to a green pasture, and in putting your child to sleep, and in writing the last line of your poem.

—*Kahlil Gibran*

• ◆ •

By engaging in a delusive quest for happiness, we bring only suffering upon ourselves. In our frantic search for something to quench our thirst, we overlook the water all around us and drive ourselves into exile from our own lives.

—*Sharon Salzberg*

The foolish man seeks happiness in the distance, the wise grows it under his feet.

—*James Oppenheim*

Happiness is not a matter of intensity but of balance, order, rhythm and harmony.

—*Thomas Merton*

Three grand essentials to happiness in this life are something to do, something to love, and something to hope for.

—*Joseph Addison*

I have chosen to be happy because it is good for my health.

—*Voltaire*

A sound mind in a sound body is a short but full description of a happy state in this world.

—*John Locke*

There is no duty we so much underrate as the duty of being happy. By being happy we sow anonymous benefits upon the world.

—*Robert Louis Stevenson*

If you want others to be happy, practice compassion. If you want to be happy, practice compassion.

—Dalai Lama

Derive happiness in oneself from a good day's work, from illuminating the fog that surrounds us.

—Henri Matisse

Dedicate yourself to the good you deserve and desire for yourself. Give yourself peace of mind. You deserve to be happy. You deserve delight.

—Hannah Arendt

Thousands of candles can be lit from a single candle, and the life of the candle will not be shortened. Happiness is never decreased by being shared.

—Buddha

There is no way to happiness, happiness is the way.

—Thich Nhat Hanh

Family and Friendship

The family is one of nature's masterpieces.

—*George Santayana*

• ◆ •

We are linked by blood, and blood is memory without language.

—*Joyce Carol Oates*

• ◆ •

In every conceivable manner, the family is link to our past, bridge to our future.

—*Alex Haley*

If you look deeply into the palm of your hand, you will see your parents and all generations of your ancestors. All of them are alive in this moment. Each is present in your body. You are the continuation of each of these people.

—*Thich Nhat Hanh*

You don't choose your family. They are God's gift to you, as you are to them.

—*Desmond Tutu*

I sustain myself with the love of family.

—*Maya Angelou*

The ideal that marriage aims at is that of spiritual union through the physical. The human love that it incarnates is intended to serve as a stepping stone to divine or universal love.

—*Mahatma Gandhi*

What greater thing is there for human souls than to feel that they are joined for life—to be with each other in silent unspeakable memories?

—*George Eliot*

Children make you want to start life over.

—*Muhammad Ali*

Genuine love not only respects the individuality of the other but actually seeks to cultivate it, even at the risk of separation or loss. The ultimate goal of life remains the spiritual growth of the individual, the solitary journey to peaks that can be climbed only alone.

—*M. Scott Peck*

• ◆ •

The most precious gift we can offer others is our presence. When mindfulness embraces those we love, they will bloom like flowers.

—*Thich Nhat Hanh*

• ◆ •

Children always challenge me to live in the present. I marvel at their ability to be fully present to me. Their uninhibited expression of affection and their willingness to receive it pull me directly into the moment and invite me to celebrate life where it is found.

—*Henri Nouwen*

• ◆ •

Parents must provide not only outer warmth for their child but also inner warmth. They must create an atmosphere with a sense of security in which the child feels love and acceptance.

—*Dalai Lama*

• ◆ •

Childrearing is above all an ethical responsibility.

—*Steven Pinker*

How would I have turned out, I sometimes wonder, had I grown up in a house that stifled enterprise by imposing harsh and senseless discipline? Or in an atmosphere of overindulgence, in a household where there were no rules, no boundaries drawn? My mother certainly understood the importance of discipline, but she always explained why some things were not allowed. Above all, she tried to be fair and to be consistent.

—*Jane Goodall*

Govern a family as you would cook a small fish—very gently.

—*Chinese proverb*

When you have children, you realize how easy it is to not see them fully, and perhaps miss all those early years. If you are not careful, you can be too absorbed in work, and they will be only too happy to tell you about it later. Being a parent is one of greatest mindfulness practices of all.

—*Jon Kabat-Zinn*

Even as we enumerate their shortcomings, the rigor of raising children ourselves makes clear to us our mothers' incredible strength. We fear both. If they are not strong, who will protect us? If they are not imperfect, how can we equal them?

—*Anna Quindlen*

Respect the child. Be not too much his parent. Trespass not on his solitude.

—*Ralph Waldo Emerson*

Our human problem—one common to parents, sons and daughters—is letting go while holding tight to the unraveling yarn that ties our hearts.

—Louise Erdrich

• ◆ •

Don't smother each other. No one can grow in the shade.

—Leo Buscaglia

• ◆ •

Mindful parenting is about moment-to-moment, openhearted and nonjudgmental attention. It's about seeing our children as they are, not as we want them to be.

—Jon Kabat-Zinn

• ◆ •

Children must be taught how to think, not what to think.

—Margaret Mead

• ◆ •

I know why families were created with all their imperfections. They humanize you. They are made to make you forget yourself occasionally, so that the beautiful balance of life is not destroyed.

—Anaïs Nin

• ◆ •

Kindness is the key to peace and harmony in family life.

—Dalai Lama

Nothing comes of so many things, if you have patience.

—*Joyce Carol Oates*

·•·

What can you do to promote world peace? Go home and love your family.

—*Mother Teresa*

·•·

There's only one thing we can be sure of, and that is the love that we have for our children, for our families, for each other. The warmth of a small child's embrace, that is true.

—*Barack Obama*

·•·

No person is your friend (or kin) who demands your silence, or denies your right to grow and be perceived as fully blossomed as you were intended.

—*Alice Walker*

·•·

Each friend represents a world in us, a world possibly not born until they arrive, and it's only by this meeting that a new world is born.

—*Anaïs Nin*

·•·

A genuine friend considers you just as another human being, as a brother or sister, and shows affection on that level, regardless of whether you are rich or poor, in a high position or a low position. That is a genuine friend.

—*Dalai Lama*

Friendship marks a life even more deeply than love. Love risks degenerating into obsession, friendship is never anything but sharing.

—Elie Wiesel

Friendship is a sheltering tree.

—Samuel Taylor Coleridge

Make yourself necessary to someone.

—Ralph Waldo Emerson

Should a seeker not find a companion who is better or equal, let them resolutely pursue a solitary course.

—Buddha

Don't walk in front of me; I may not follow. Don't walk behind me; I may not lead. Just walk beside me and be my friend.

—Albert Camus

We should always have three friends in our lives: one who walks ahead, who we look up to and follow; one who walks beside us, who is with us every step of our journey; and then, one who we reach back for and bring along after we've cleared the way.

—Michelle Obama

Friendship is the source of the greatest pleasures, and without friends even the most agreeable pursuits become tedious.

—St. Thomas Aquinas

Friendship improves happiness and abates misery, by the doubling of our joy and the dividing of our grief.

—Cicero

For without friends, no one would choose to live, though he had all other goods.

—Aristotle

If you're someone people count on, particularly in difficult moments, that's a sign of a life lived honorably.

—Rachel Maddow

One of the most beautiful qualities of true friendship is to understand and to be understood.

—Seneca

Obstacles and Challenges

Life is difficult. This is a great truth, one of the greatest truths. It is a great truth because once we truly see this truth, we transcend it. Once we truly know that life is difficult—once we truly understand and accept it—then life is no longer difficult. Because once it is accepted, the fact that life is difficult no longer matters.

—*M. Scott Peck*

• ◆ •

If we can really understand the problem, the answer will come out of it, because the answer is not separate from the problem.

—*Jiddu Krishnamurti*

• ◆ •

If we are facing the right direction, all we have to do is keep on walking.

—*Buddhist proverb*

I was taught that the way of progress is neither swift nor easy.

—*Marie Curie*

• ◆ •

Man needs difficulties; they are necessary for health.

—*Carl Jung*

• ◆ •

Were it not for my little jokes, I could not bear the burdens of this office.

—*Abraham Lincoln*

• ◆ •

Humor is just another defense against the universe.

—*Mel Brooks*

• ◆ •

Life is not easy for any of us. But what of that? We must have perseverance and above all confidence in ourselves. We must believe that we are gifted for something, and that this thing, at whatever cost, must be attained.

—*Marie Curie*

• ◆ •

I read my own books sometimes to cheer me when it is hard to write, and then I remember that it was always difficult, and how nearly impossible it was sometimes.

—*Ernest Hemingway*

Anyone who has never made a mistake has never tried anything new.

                                  —*Albert Einstein*

•◆•

To make no mistake is not in the power of man; but from their errors and mistakes the wise and good learn wisdom for the future.

                                         —*Plutarch*

•◆•

When I have listened to my mistakes, I have grown.

                                  —*Hugh Prather*

•◆•

My great concern is not whether you have failed, but whether you are content with your failure.

                                 —*Abraham Lincoln*

•◆•

A man who has committed a mistake and doesn't correct it is committing another mistake.

                                 —*Confucius*

•◆•

Finite to fail, but infinite to venture.

                                 —*Emily Dickinson*

•◆•

Our greatest glory is not in never falling, but in rising every time we fall.

                                 —*Oliver Goldsmith*

When I dare to be powerful, to use my strength in the service of my vision, then it becomes less and less important whether I am afraid.

—Audre Lorde

• ◆ •

Inside of a ring or not, ain't nothing wrong with going down. It's staying down that's wrong.

—Muhammad Ali

• ◆ •

Failure is the foundation of success, and the means by which it is achieved.

—Lao Tzu

• ◆ •

The probability that we may fail in the struggle ought not to deter us from the support of a cause we believe to be just.

—Abraham Lincoln

• ◆ •

Good people are good because they've come to wisdom through failure.

—William Saroyan

Suffering, Hardship, and Loss

Life is suffering.

—Buddha

My soul is a broken field, plowed by pain.

—Sara Teasdale

Tears are the prayer-beads of all of us, men and women, because they arise from a fullness of the heart.

—Father Edward Hays

In this sad world of ours, sorrow comes to all; and to the young, it comes with bitterest agony, because it takes them unawares.

—Abraham Lincoln

It is from pain and our own limits where we best learn to grow, and from our own flaws surges the deep question: haven't we suffered enough to decide to break old patterns?

—*Pope Francis*

• • •

When another person makes you suffer, it is because he suffers deeply within himself, and his suffering is spilling over. He does not need punishment; he needs help. That's the message he is sending.

—*Thich Nhat Hanh*

• • •

Things falling apart is a kind of testing and also a kind of healing.

—*Pema Chödrön*

• • •

We must embrace pain and burn it as fuel for our journey.

—*Kenji Miyazawa*

• • •

Don't turn away. Keep your gaze on the bandaged place. That's where the light enters you.

—*Rumi*

• • •

Without the burden of afflictions it is impossible to reach the height of grace. The gift of grace increases as the struggles increase.

—*St. Rose of Lima*

Suffering begins to dissolve when we can question the belief or the hope that there's anywhere to hide.

—*Pema Chödrön*

＊◆＊

The attempt to avoid legitimate suffering lies at the root of all emotional illness.

—*M. Scott Peck*

＊◆＊

Deep unspeakable suffering may well be called a baptism, a regeneration, the initiation into a new state.

—*George Eliot*

＊◆＊

There are some things you learn best in calm, and some in storm.

—*Willa Cather*

＊◆＊

Pain is never permanent.

—*St. Teresa of Avila*

＊◆＊

Pain is the root of knowledge.

—*Simone Weil*

＊◆＊

Nothing ever goes away until it has taught us what we need to know.

—*Pema Chödrön*

The truth that many people never understand, until it is too late, is that the more you try to avoid suffering the more you suffer because smaller and more insignificant things begin to torture you in proportion to your fear of being hurt.

—*Thomas Merton*

If all misfortunes were laid in one common heap whence everyone must take an equal portion, most people would be contented to take their own and depart.

—*Socrates*

The world is full of suffering, it is also full of the overcoming of it.

—*Helen Keller*

True knowledge comes only through suffering.

—*Elizabeth Barrett Browning*

Do not despair of life. You have no doubt force enough to overcome your obstacles.

—*Henry David Thoreau*

I give myself a good cry if I need it, but then I concentrate on all good things still in my life.

—*Mitch Albom*

You are not your illness. You have an individual story to tell. You have a name, a history, a personality. Staying yourself is part of the battle.

—Julian Seifter

• ◆ •

Difficult times have helped me to understand better than before how infinitely rich and beautiful life is in every way and that so many things that one goes worrying about are of no importance whatsoever.

—Isak Dinesen

• ◆ •

The most beautiful people we have known are those who have known defeat, known suffering, known struggle, known loss, and have found their way out of the depths. These persons have an appreciation, a sensitivity, and an understanding of life that fills them with compassion, gentleness, and a deep loving concern. Beautiful people do not just happen.

—Elisabeth Kübler-Ross

• ◆ •

The gem cannot be polished without friction, nor man perfected without trials.

—Confucius

• ◆ •

Those who have suffered understand suffering and therefore extend their hand.

—Patti Smith

And once the storm is over, you won't remember how you made it through, how you managed to survive. You won't even be sure whether the storm is really over. But one thing is certain. When you come out of the storm, you won't be the same person who walked in. That's what this storm's all about.

—*Haruki Murakami*

I do not believe that sheer suffering teaches. If suffering alone taught, all the world would be wise, since everyone suffers. To suffering must be added mourning, understanding, patience, love, openness and the willingness to remain vulnerable.

—*Anne Morrow Lindbergh*

Courage doesn't always roar. Sometimes courage is the little voice at the end of the day that says I'll try again tomorrow.

—*Mary Anne Radmacher*

The world breaks everyone, and afterward, some are strong at the broken places.

—*Ernest Hemingway*

When you are sorrowful look again in your heart, and you shall see that in truth you are weeping for that which has been your delight.

—*Kahlil Gibran*

There are as many nights as days, and the one is just as long as the other in the year's course. Even a happy life cannot be without a measure of darkness, and the word "happy" would lose its meaning if it were not balanced by sadness.

—Carl Jung

• ◆ •

That which does not kill me makes me stronger.

—Friedrich Nietzsche

• ◆ •

In the depth of winter, I finally learned that there was within me an invincible summer.

—Albert Camus

• ◆ •

Grief can be the garden of compassion. If you keep your heart open through everything, your pain can become your greatest ally in your life's search for love and wisdom.

—Rumi

• ◆ •

If we could see that everything, even tragedy, is a gift in disguise, we would then find the best way to nourish the soul.

—Elisabeth Kübler-Ross

Grief drives men into habits of serious reflection, sharpens the understanding and softens the heart.

—John Quincy Adams

Unable are the loved to die. For love is immortality.

—Emily Dickinson

It isn't for the moment you are stuck that you need courage, but for the long uphill climb back to sanity and faith and security.

—Anne Morrow Lindbergh

The deeper that sorrow carves into your being the more joy you can contain. Is not the cup that holds your wine the very cup that was burned in the potter's oven?

—Kahlil Gibran

Affliction comes to us all not to make us sad, but sober; not to make us sorry, but wise; not to make us despondent, but by its darkness to refresh us, as the night refreshes the day; not to impoverish, but to enrich us, as the plough enriches the field; to multiply our joy, as the seed by planting is multiplied a thousand-fold.

—Henry Ward Beecher

Death, when it approaches, ought not to take one by surprise.
It should be part of the full expectancy of life.

—*Muriel Spark*

For what is it to die but to stand naked in the wind and to melt
into the sun? And what is it to cease breathing, but to free the
breath from its restless tides, that it may rise and expand and
seek God unencumbered?

—*Kahlil Gibran*

Gratitude and Hope

When I first open my eyes upon the morning meadows and look out upon the beautiful world, I thank God I am alive.

—*Ralph Waldo Emerson*

•◆•

The best things are nearest: breath in your nostrils, light in your eyes, flowers at your feet, duties at your hand, the path of God just before you. Then do not grasp at the stars, but do life's plain, common work as it comes, certain that daily duties and daily bread are the sweetest things of life.

—*Robert Louis Stevenson*

•◆•

Just to be is a blessing, just to live is holy.

—*Rabbi Abraham Joshua Heschel*

Why do some people always see beautiful skies and grass and lovely flowers and incredible human beings, while others are hard-pressed to find anything or any place that is beautiful?

—Leo Buscaglia

•◆•

So much has been given to me; I have not time to ponder over that which has been denied.

—Helen Keller

•◆•

Reflect upon your blessings, of which every man has plenty, not on your past misfortunes, of which all men have some.

—Charles Dickens

•◆•

I like living. I have sometimes been wildly, despairingly, acutely miserable, racked with sorrow, but through it all I still know quite certainly that just to be alive is a grand thing.

—Agatha Christie

•◆•

If you concentrate on finding whatever is good in every situation, you will discover that your life will suddenly be filled with gratitude, a feeling that nurtures the soul.

—Rabbi Harold Kushner

•◆•

Abundance is not something we acquire. It is something we tune into.

—Wayne Dyer

Be glad of life, because it gives you the chance to love, and to work, and to play and to look up at the stars.

—Henry Van Dyke

Gratitude is not only the greatest of virtues, but the parent of all the others.

—Cicero

We can be thankful to a friend for a few acres or a little money; and yet for the freedom and command of the whole earth, and for the great benefits of our being, our life, health, and reason, we look upon ourselves as under no obligation.

—Seneca

We often take for granted the very things that most deserve our gratitude.

—Cynthia Ozick

I am grateful for what I am and have. My thanksgiving is perpetual. It is surprising how contented one can be with nothing definite— only a sense of existence. My breath is sweet to me. O how I laugh when I think of my vague indefinite riches. No run on my bank can drain it, for my wealth is not possession but enjoyment.

—Henry David Thoreau

There is a calmness to a life lived in gratitude, a quiet joy.

—*Ralph H. Blum*

• ◆ •

I am thankful that thus far today I have not had any unkind thoughts or said any harsh words or done anything that I regret. However, now I need to get out of bed and so things may become more difficult.

—*Sylvia Boorstein*

• ◆ •

Acknowledging the good that you already have in your life is the foundation for all abundance.

—*Eckhart Tolle*

• ◆ •

Think of the ills from which you are exempt.

—*Joseph Joubert*

• ◆ •

Every day, tell at least one person something you like, admire, or appreciate about them.

—*Richard Carlson*

• ◆ •

Silent gratitude isn't very much to anyone.

—*Gertrude Stein*

Do not spoil what you have by desiring what you have not;
remember that what you now have was once among the things
you only hoped for.

—*Epicurus*

• ◆ •

The best way to not feel hopeless is to get up and do something.
Don't wait for good things to happen to you. If you go out and
make some good things happen, you will fill the world with
hope, you will fill yourself with hope.

—*Barack Obama*

• ◆ •

We do not need magic to change the world, we carry all the power we
need inside ourselves already: we have the power to imagine better.

—*J. K. Rowling*

• ◆ •

Once you choose hope anything is possible.

—*Christopher Reeve*

• ◆ •

Hope begins in the dark, the stubborn hope that if you just
show up and try to do the right thing, the dawn will come.
You wait and watch and work: you don't give up.

—*Anne Lamott*

• ◆ •

Desire and hope will push us on toward the future.

—*Montaigne*

Hope is a very unruly emotion.

—Gloria Steinem

• ◆ •

Hope is being able to see that there is light despite all of the darkness.

—Desmond Tutu

• ◆ •

When you get into a tight place and everything goes against you, till it seems as though you could not hang on a minute longer, never give up then, for that is just the place and time that the tide will turn.

—Harriet Beecher Stowe

• ◆ •

Hope is important because it can make the present moment less difficult to bear. If we believe that tomorrow will be better, we can bear a hardship today.

—Thich Nhat Hanh

• ◆ •

Hope is like a road in the country; there was never a road, but when many people walk on it, the road comes into existence.

—Lin Yutang

• ◆ •

Where there's life, there's hope.

—Terence

We must accept finite disappointment, but never lose infinite hope.

—Martin Luther King Jr.

•—•

All human wisdom is summed up in two words; wait and hope.

—Alexandre Dumas

Our Shared Humanity

My humanity is bound up in yours, for we can only be human together.

—Desmond Tutu

• ◆ •

Nobody, but nobody
Can make it out here alone.

—Maya Angelou

• ◆ •

In the faces of men and women I see God, and in my own face in the glass.

—Walt Whitman

All of us failed to match our dreams of perfection.

—*William Faulkner*

. •• .

You have your way. I have my way. As for the right way,
the correct way, and the only way, it does not exist.

—*Friedrich Nietzsche*

. •• .

We have a tendency to condemn people who are different from
us, to define their sins as paramount and our own sinfulness as
being insignificant.

—*Jimmy Carter*

. •• .

If we learn to open our hearts, anyone, including the people who
drive us crazy, can be our teacher.

—*Pema Chödrön*

. •• .

What is tolerance? It is the consequence of humanity. We are all
formed of frailty and error; let us pardon reciprocally each other's
folly—that is the first law of nature.

—*Voltaire*

. •• .

One of the first things to learn if you want to be a contemplative is
to mind your own business. Nothing is more suspicious, in a man
who seems holy, than an impatient desire to reform other men.

—*Thomas Merton*

Whenever you're in conflict with someone, there is one factor that can make the difference between damaging your relationship and deepening it. That factor is attitude.

—William James

· ◆ ·

Every time a man unburdens his heart to a stranger he reaffirms the love that unites humanity.

—Germaine Greer

· ◆ ·

The person who tries to live alone will not succeed as a human being. His heart withers if it does not answer another heart. His mind shrinks away if he hears only the echoes of his own thoughts and finds no other inspiration.

—Pearl S. Buck

· ◆ ·

The brain is a social organ, and our relationships with one another are not a luxury but an essential nutrient for our survival.

—Daniel J. Siegel

· ◆ ·

The presence of others who see what we see and hear what we hear assures us of the reality of the world and ourselves.

—Hannah Arendt

· ◆ ·

Speak your truth quietly and clearly; and listen to others, even to the dull and the ignorant; they too have their story.

—Max Ehrmann

Everything that irritates us about others can lead us to an understanding of ourselves.

—Carl Jung

．→・

Just as true humor is laughter at oneself, true humanity is knowledge of oneself.

—Alan Watts

．→・

It is a glorious destiny to be a member of the human race, though it is a race dedicated to many absurdities and one which makes many terrible mistakes.

—Thomas Merton

．→・

Human nature is potentially aggressive and destructive and potentially orderly and constructive.

—Margaret Mead

．→・

I keep my ideals, because in spite of everything I still believe that people are really good at heart.

—Anne Frank

．→・

You must not lose faith in humanity. Humanity is an ocean; if a few drops of the ocean are dirty, the ocean does not become dirty.

—Mahatma Gandhi

Everyone has his own specific vocation or mission in life;
everyone must carry out a concrete assignment that demands
fulfillment. Therein he cannot be replaced, nor can his life
be repeated, thus, everyone's task is unique as his specific
opportunity to implement it.

—*Viktor E. Frankl*

Our true nature is like a precious jewel: although it may be
temporarily buried in mud, it remains completely brilliant and
unaffected. We simply have to uncover it.

—*Pema Chödrön*

In everyone's life, at some time, our inner fire goes out. It is then
burst into flame by an encounter with another human being. We
should all be thankful for those people who rekindle our inner spirit.

—*Albert Schweitzer*

It really boils down to this: that all life is interrelated. We are all
caught in an inescapable network of mutuality, tied in a single
garment of destiny. Whatever affects one directly, affects all
indirectly.

—*Martin Luther King Jr.*

Our human compassion binds us the one to the other—not in pity or patronizingly, but as human beings who have learnt how to turn our common suffering into hope for the future.

—Nelson Mandela

. ❖ .

If we are to achieve a richer culture, rich in contrasting values, we must recognize the whole gamut of human potentialities, and so weave a less arbitrary social fabric, one in which each diverse human gift will find a fitting place.

—Margaret Mead

. ❖ .

We become not a melting pot but a beautiful mosaic. Different people, different beliefs, different yearnings, different hopes, different dreams.

—Jimmy Carter

. ❖ .

No man is an island entire of itself. Each is a piece of the continent, a part of the main.

—John Donne

. ❖ .

When watching after yourself, you watch after others. When watching after others, you watch after yourself.

—Buddha

You are whole and also part of larger and larger circles of
wholeness you many not even know about. You are never alone.
And you already belong. You belong to humanity. You belong to
life. You belong to this moment, this breath.

—*Jon Kabat-Zinn*

◦◆◦

We must learn to live together as brothers or perish together
as fools.

—*Martin Luther King Jr.*

◦◆◦

Our responsibility is much greater than we might have supposed,
because it involves all mankind.

—*Jean-Paul Sartre*

◦◆◦

We know that every moment is a moment of grace, every
hour is an offering; not to share them would be to betray them.
Our lives no longer belong to us alone; they belong to all those
who need us desperately.

—*Elie Wiesel*

◦◆◦

If we have no peace, it is because we have forgotten that we
belong to each other.

—*Mother Teresa*

The Beauty and
Wonder of Life

Beauty and grace are performed whether or not we will or sense them. The least we can try to do is be there.

—*Annie Dillard*

One way to open your eyes to unnoticed beauty is to ask yourself, "What if I had never seen this before? What if I knew I would never see it again?"

—*Rachel Carson*

Look at everything always as though you were seeing it either for the first or last time: Thus is your time on earth filled with glory.

—*Betty Smith*

I was not looking now at an unusual flower arrangement. I was
seeing what Adam had seen on the morning of his creation—
the miracle, moment by moment of naked existence.

—*Aldous Huxley*

• ◆ •

The real voyage of discovery consists not in seeking new
landscapes, but in having new eyes.

—*Marcel Proust*

• ◆ •

Some people feel the rain. Others just get wet.

—*Bob Marley*

• ◆ •

The main thing is that you hear life's music everywhere.
Most people hear only its dissonances.

—*Theodor Fontane*

• ◆ •

All the things that truly matter, beauty, love, creativity, joy and
inner peace arise from beyond the mind.

—*Eckhart Tolle*

• ◆ •

You are not a drop in the ocean,
You are the entire ocean in a drop.

—*Rumi*

Wake up and Live!

—*Bob Marley*

.•.

The kingdom of God is within you.

—*Luke 17:21*

.•.

I wish I could show you when you are lonely or in darkness,
the Astonishing Light of your own being.

—*Hafiz of Shiraz*

.•.

Let the beauty we love be what we do; there are hundreds of
ways to kneel and kiss the ground.

—*Rumi*

.•.

Truly, we live with mysteries too marvelous
     to be understood. . .
Let me keep my distance, always, from those
     who think they have the answers.
Let me keep company always with those who say
     "Look!" and laugh in astonishment,
     and bow their heads.

—*Mary Oliver*

.•.

Those who contemplate the beauty of the earth find reserves of
strength that will endure as long as life lasts.

—*Rachel Carson*

Looking at beauty in the world is the first step of purifying the mind.

—*Amit Ray*

• ◆ •

Life is better than death, I believe, if only because it is less boring, and because it has fresh peaches in it.

—*Alice Walker*

• ◆ •

I don't think of all the misery, but of the beauty that still remains.

—*Anne Frank*

• ◆ •

Among all things that are lovable, there is one that is more lovable than the rest, and that most lovable of all things is life.

—*St. Anthony of Padua*

• ◆ •

The human heart yearns for the beautiful in all ranks of life.

—*Harriet Beecher Stowe*

• ◆ •

There are only two ways to live your life. One is as though nothing is a miracle. The other is as though everything is a miracle.

—*Albert Einstein*

Commune with Nature

An early morning walk is a blessing for the whole day.

—Henry David Thoreau

⚫◆⚫

I believe a leaf of grass is no less than the journey-work of the stars.

—Walt Whitman

⚫◆⚫

The moment one gives close attention to anything, even a blade of grass, it becomes a mysterious, awesome, indescribably magnificent world in itself.

—Henry Miller

To the dull mind nature is leaden. To the illumined mind
the whole world burns and sparkles with light.

—Ralph Waldo Emerson

. ◆ .

Sunshine is delicious, rain is refreshing, wind braces us up,
snow is exhilarating; there is really no such thing as bad weather,
only different kinds of good weather.

—John Ruskin

. ◆ .

Rain is grace; rain is the sky condescending to the earth;
without rain, there would be no life.

—John Updike

. ◆ .

The birds have vanished into the sky, and now the last cloud
    drains away.
We sit together, the mountain and me, until only the mountain
    remains.

—Li Po

. ◆ .

Nothing is rich but the inexhaustible wealth of nature.
She shows us only surfaces, but she is a million fathoms deep.

—Ralph Waldo Emerson

. ◆ .

You will find something more in woods than in books. Trees and
stones will teach you that which you can never learn from masters.

—St. Bernard of Clairvaux

If we could see the miracle of a single flower clearly, our whole life would change.

—Buddha

Nature's peace will flow into you as sunshine flows into trees. The winds will blow their own freshness into you, and the storms their energy, while cares will drop off like autumn leaves.

—John Muir

Listening to the birds can be a meditation if you listen with awareness.

—Osho

I think it annoys God if you walk by the color purple in a field and don't notice.

—Alice Walker

I once had a sparrow alight on my shoulder for a moment while I was hoeing in a village garden, and I felt that I was more distinguished by that circumstance than I should have been by any epaulet I could have worn.

—Henry David Thoreau

What a joy it is to feel the soft, springy earth under my feet once more, to follow grassy roads that lead to ferny brooks where I can bathe my fingers in a cataract of rippling notes, or to clamber over a stone wall into green fields that tumble and roll and climb in riotous gladness!

—*Helen Keller*

This grand show is eternal. It is always sunrise somewhere; the dew is never all dried at once; a shower is forever falling; vapor is ever rising. Eternal sunrise, eternal sunset, eternal dawn and gloaming, on sea and continents and islands, each in its turn, as the round earth rolls.

—*John Muir*

The best remedy for those who are afraid, lonely or unhappy is to go outside, somewhere where they can be quiet, alone with the heavens, nature and God. Because only then does one feel that all is as it should be.

—*Anne Frank*

No man should go through life without once experiencing healthy, even bored solitude in the wilderness, finding himself depending solely on himself and thereby learning his true and hidden strength.

—*Jack Kerouac*

I need to be alone. I need to ponder my shame and my despair in
seclusion; I need the sunshine and the paving stones of the streets
without companions, without conversation, face to face with
myself, with only the music of my heart for company.

—*Henry Miller*

Today, more than ever before, life must be characterized by a
sense of universal responsibility, not only nation to nation and
human to human, but also human to other forms of life.

—*Dalai Lama*

And forget not that the earth delights to feel your bare feet
and the winds long to play with your hair.

—*Kahlil Gibran*

You are a function of what the whole universe is doing
in the same way that a wave is a function of what the whole
ocean is doing.

—*Alan Watts*

The old Lakota was wise. He knew that man's heart away from
nature becomes hard; he knew that lack of respect for growing,
living things soon led to lack of respect for humans, too.

—*Luther Standing Bear*

The deeper we look into nature, the more we recognize that it is full of life, and the more profoundly we know that all life is a secret and that we are united with all life that is in nature. Man can no longer live his life for himself alone. We realize that all life is valuable and that we are united to all this life. From this knowledge comes our spiritual relationship with the universe.

—Albert Schweitzer

．◆．

But I'll tell you what hermits realize. If you go off into a far, far forest and get very quiet, you'll come to understand that you're connected with everything.

—Alan Watts

．◆．

As people alive today, we must consider future generations: a clean environment is a human right like any other. It is therefore part of our responsibility toward others to ensure that the world we pass on is as healthy, if not healthier, than we found it.

—Dalai Lama

．◆．

Anyone who tries to improve the lives of animals invariably comes in for criticism from those who believe such efforts are misplaced in a world of suffering humanity.

—Jane Goodall

As a bee gathering nectar does not harm or disturb the color and fragrance of the flower; so do the wise move through the world.

—*Buddha*

. ✦ .

The sage has the sun and moon by his side. He grasps the universe under the arm. He blends everything into a harmonious whole, casts aside whatever is confused or obscured, and regards the humble as honourable.

—*Chuang Tzu*

. ✦ .

After you have exhausted what there is in business, politics, conviviality, and so on—have found that none of these finally satisfy, or permanently wear—what remains? Nature remains.

—*Walt Whitman*

Spirituality and Prayer

We are not human beings having a spiritual experience.
We are spiritual beings having a human experience.

—*Pierre Teilhard de Chardin*

• ◆ •

It is this belief in a power larger than myself and other than
myself which allows me to venture into the unknown and even
the unknowable.

—*Maya Angelou*

• ◆ •

That is the religious experience: the astonishment of meeting
someone who is waiting for you.

—*Pope Francis*

We can bring our spiritual practice into the streets, into our communities, when we see each realm as a temple, as a place to discover that which is sacred.

—*Jack Kornfield*

A life is either all spiritual or not spiritual at all. No man can serve two masters. Your life is shaped by the end you live for. You are made in the image of what you desire.

—*Thomas Merton*

Spirituality doesn't look like sitting down and meditating. Spirituality looks like folding the towels in a sweet way and talking kindly to the people in the family even though you've had a rough day.

—*Sylvia Boorstein*

Zen does not confuse spirituality with thinking about God while one is peeling potatoes. Zen spirituality is just to peel the potatoes.

—*Alan Watts*

Faith does not contradict reason but transcends it.

—*Mahatma Gandhi*

To one who has faith, no explanation is necessary. To one without faith, no explanation is possible.

—*St. Thomas Aquinas*

Faith is different from proof; the latter is human, the former is a Gift from God.

—*Blaise Pascal*

. ✦ .

Doubt isn't the opposite of faith; it is an element of faith.

—*Paul Tillich*

. ✦ .

Take the first step in faith. You don't have to see the whole staircase, just take the first step.

—*Martin Luther King Jr.*

. ✦ .

Gentleness, self-sacrifice and generosity are the exclusive possession of no one race or religion.

—*Mahatma Gandhi*

. ✦ .

This is my simple religion. There is no need for temples; no need for complicated philosophy. Our own brain, our own heart is our temple; the philosophy is kindness.

—*Dalai Lama*

. ✦ .

I never told my religion nor scrutinized that of another. I never attempted to make a convert nor wished to change another's creed. I have judged of others' religion by their lives, for it is from our lives and not from our words that our religion must be read.

—*Thomas Jefferson*

Whenever violence is done in the name of religion, we must make it clear to everyone that in such instances we are not dealing with true religion.

—*St. John Paul II*

• ◆ •

Spirituality is recognizing the divine light that is within us all. It doesn't belong to any particular religion; it belongs to everyone.

—*Muhammad Ali*

• ◆ •

We do not weary of eating and sleeping every day, for hunger and sleepiness recur. Without that we should weary of them. So, without the hunger for spiritual things, we weary of them.

—*Blaise Pascal*

• ◆ •

Today, humanity is bowed down with trouble, sorrow and grief, no one escapes; the world is wet with tears; but, thank God, the remedy is at our doors. Let us turn our hands away from the world of matter and live in the spiritual world.

—*Abdul Baha*

• ◆ •

I love you when you bow in your mosque, kneel in your temple, pray in your church. For you and I are sons of one religion, and it is the spirit.

—*Kahlil Gibran*

All major religious traditions carry basically the same message, that is love, compassion and forgiveness…the important thing is they should be part of our daily lives.

—Dalai Lama

Prayer is the song of the heart. It reaches the ear of God even if it is mingled with the cry and tumult of a thousand men.

—Kahlil Gibran

Miracles happen. But prayer is needed! Prayer that is courageous, struggling, and persevering, not prayer that is a mere formality.

—Pope Francis

Prayer is not asking. It is a longing of the soul.

—Mahatma Gandhi

The sovereign cure for worry is prayer.

—William James

Prayer is not asking. Prayer is putting oneself in the hands of God, at his disposition, and listening to his voice in the depths of our hearts.

—Mother Teresa

There is guidance for each of us, and by lowly listening,
we shall hear the right word.

—*Ralph Waldo Emerson*

Everything that one turns in the direction of God is a prayer.

—*St. Ignatius of Loyola*

An authentic life is the most personal form of worship.
Everyday life has become my prayer.

—*Sarah Ban Breathnach*

If the only prayer you said in your whole life was, "thank you,"
that would suffice.

—*Meister Eckhart*

The aim of spiritual life is to awaken a joyful freedom, a
benevolent and compassionate heart in spite of everything.

—*Jack Kornfield*

God speaks in the silence of the heart. Listening is the beginning
of prayer.

—*Mother Teresa*

Sanctify yourself and you will sanctify society.

—*St. Francis of Assisi*

•◆•

At any moment, you have a choice, that either leads you closer to your spirit or further away from it.

—*Thich Nhat Hanh*

Becoming Your Best Self

Today, you can decide to walk in freedom. You can choose
to walk differently. You can walk as a free person, enjoying
every step.

—Thich Nhat Hanh

• ◆ •

At the center of your being you have the answer; you know who
you are, and you know what you want.

—Lao Tzu

• ◆ •

We must look at our life without sentimentality, exaggeration
or idealism. Does what we are choosing reflect what we most
deeply value?

—Jack Kornfield

The more honest one is, the easier it is to continue being honest, just as the more lies one has told, the more necessary it is to lie again. By their openness, people dedicated to the truth live in the open, and through the exercise of their courage to live in the open, they become free from fear.

—M. Scott Peck

. ◆ .

Without giving up hope—that there's somewhere better to be, that there's someone better to be—we will never relax with where we are or who we are.

—Pema Chödrön

. ◆ .

The thing that is really hard, and really amazing, is giving up on being perfect and beginning the work of becoming yourself.

—Anna Quindlen

. ◆ .

Part of spiritual and emotional maturity is recognizing that it's not like you're going to try to fix yourself and become a different person. You remain the same person, but you become awakened.

—Jack Kornfield

. ◆ .

You have a treasure within you that is infinitely greater than anything the world can offer.

—Eckhart Tolle

We each need to let our intuition guide us, and then be willing to follow that guidance directly and fearlessly.

—Shakti Gawain

•◆•

Should you find a wise critic to point out your faults, follow him as you would a guide to hidden treasure.

—Buddha

•◆•

Men go abroad to admire the heights of mountains, the mighty waves of the sea, the broad tides of rivers, the compass of the ocean, and the circuits of the stars, yet pass over the mystery of themselves without a thought.

—St. Augustine

•◆•

By breaking down our sense of self-importance, all we lose is a parasite that has long infected our minds. What we gain in return is freedom, openness of mind, spontaneity, simplicity, altruism: all qualities inherent in happiness.

—Matthieu Ricard

•◆•

We are always in a perpetual state of being created and creating ourselves.

—Daniel J. Siegel

The most common way people give up their power is by thinking they don't have any.

—*Alice Walker*

•◆•

We are not yet what we shall be, but we are growing toward it, the process is not yet finished.

—*Martin Luther*

•◆•

We are all teachers and students of ourselves.

—*A. Bartlett Giamatti*

•◆•

By oneself is evil done; by oneself is one defiled. By oneself is evil left undone; by oneself is one made pure. Purity and impurity depend on oneself; no one can purify another.

—*Buddha*

•◆•

To follow the path, look to the master, follow the master, walk with the master, see through the master, become the master.

—*Zen proverb*

•◆•

It isn't until you come to a spiritual understanding of who you are—not necessarily a religious feeling, but deep down, the spirit within—that you can begin to take control.

—*Oprah Winfrey*

Never think that someone else knows what's best for you.
Trust your way and don't ask for so much advice. Learn how
to be quiet and still enough to hear your own voice. It's up to
you: Your voice will either be silenced or will get to roar.

—*Maria Shriver*

Just trust yourself, then you will know how to live.

—*Goethe*

The greatest danger, that of losing one's own self, may pass off
quietly as if it were nothing; every other loss, that of an arm, a
leg, five dollars, etc., is sure to be noticed.

—*Søren Kierkegaard*

Western laziness consists of cramming our lives with compulsive
activity, so that there is no time at all to confront the real issues.

—*Sogyal Rinpoche*

If a man is to live, he must be all alive, body, soul, mind, heart,
spirit.

—*Thomas Merton*

We all need to have a creative outlet—a window, a space—so we
don't lose track of ourselves.

—*Norman Fischer*

I believed what I was told and not what my own eyes saw.

—*Margaret Drabble*

. ◆ .

Why should we be in such desperate haste to succeed, and in such desperate enterprises? If a man does not keep pace with his companions, perhaps it is because he hears a different drummer.

—*Henry David Thoreau*

. ◆ .

Experience life in all possible ways—good-bad, bitter-sweet, dark-light, summer-winter. Experience all the dualities. Don't be afraid of experience, because the more experience you have, the more mature you become.

—*Osho*

. ◆ .

How can you know what you're capable of if you don't embrace the unknown?

—*Esmeralda Santiago*

. ◆ .

To be what we are, and to become what we are capable of becoming, is the only end of life.

—*Robert Louis Stevenson*

. ◆ .

We do the best we can with what we have and when we know better, we do better.

—*Maya Angelou*

Figuring out who you are is the whole point of the human experience.

—*Anna Quindlen*

I've come to believe that each of us has a personal calling that's as unique as a fingerprint—and that the best way to succeed is to discover what you love and then find a way to offer it to others in the form of service, working hard, and also allowing the energy of the universe to lead you.

—*Oprah Winfrey*

Promise me you'll always remember—you're braver than you believe, stronger than you seem and smarter than you think.

—*A. A. Milne*

Our true nature is not some deal that we have to live up to. It's who we are right now, and that's what we can make friends with and celebrate.

—*Pema Chödrön*

The human race is challenged more than ever before to demonstrate our mastery—not over nature but of ourselves.

—*Rachel Carson*

It all depends on you. You can go on sleeping forever, you can wake up right this moment.

—*Osho*

⋅◆⋅

Yesterday I was clever, so I wanted to change the world.
Today I am wise, so I am changing myself.

—*Rumi*

Mindful Wisdom

When you arise in the morning, think of what a privilege it is to be alive—to breathe, to think, to enjoy, to love.

—*Marcus Aurelius*

To live is not merely to breathe, it is to act; it is to make use of our organs, senses, faculties, of all those parts of ourselves which give us the feeling of existence.

—*Jean-Jacques Rousseau*

I have just three things to teach: simplicity, patience, compassion. These three are your greatest treasures.

—*Lao Tzu*

When somebody's living mindfully, they're really being there;
as opposed to half-there or multitasking or paying attention to
three things at once.

—*Judson Brewer*

•—◆—•

Your mind is your instrument. Learn to be its master and not
its slave.

—*Remez Sasson*

•—◆—•

When we go beyond the superficial and conventional
understandings of our habitual patterns, when we look
deeper and enlarge the scope of our vision, we develop a wiser
relationship with all aspects of our experience.

—*Oprah Winfrey*

•—◆—•

If something is boring after two minutes, try it for four. If still
boring, try it for eight, sixteen, thirty-two, and so on. Eventually,
one discovers that it is not boring but very interesting.

—*Zen saying*

•—◆—•

All of man's difficulties are caused by his inability to sit, quietly,
in a room by himself.

—*Blaise Pascal*

You should sit in meditation for twenty minutes every day—
unless you are too busy—then you should sit for an hour.

—*Buddhist proverb*

•◆•

As long as one keeps searching, the answers come.

—*Joan Baez*

•◆•

It is never too late to be what you might have been.

—*George Eliot*

•◆•

Eternity is not something that begins after you are dead.
It is going on all the time. We are in it now.

—*Charlotte Perkins Gilman*

•◆•

Don't worry about what the world needs. Ask what makes you
come alive and do that. Because what the world needs is people
who have come alive.

—*Howard Thurman*

•◆•

Life can only be understood backward, but it must be lived forward.

—*Søren Kierkegaard*

•◆•

Believe that life is worth living and your belief will help create
the fact.

—*William James*

The only true guardian of peace lies within: a sense of concern and responsibility for your own future and an altruistic concern for the well-being of others.

—*Dalai Lama*

• ◆ •

I wish that life should not be cheap, but sacred. I wish the days to be as centuries, loaded, fragrant.

—*Ralph Waldo Emerson*

• ◆ •

Learn to be pleased with everything; with wealth, so far as it makes us beneficial to others; with poverty, for not having much to care for; and with obscurity, for being unenvied.

—*Plutarch*

• ◆ •

It is said an Eastern monarch once charged his wise men to invent him a sentence to be ever in view, and which should be true and appropriate in all times and situations. They presented him the words: "And this, too, shall pass away." How much it expresses! How chastening in the hour of pride! How consoling in the depths of affliction!

—*Abraham Lincoln*

• ◆ •

In the end, just three things matter: How well we have lived. How well we have loved. How well we have learned to let go.

—*Jack Kornfield*

In dwelling, live close to the ground. In thinking, keep to the simple. In conflict, be fair and generous. In governing, don't try to control. In work, do what you enjoy. In family life, be completely present.

—*Lao Tzu*

Do what you can, with what you have, where you are.

—*Theodore Roosevelt*

When we are unhurried and wise we perceive that only great and worthy things have any permanent and absolute existence— that petty fears and petty pleasures are but the shadow of reality. This is always exhilarating and sublime.

—*Henry David Thoreau*

We do not discover new lands without consenting to lose sight of the shore for a very long time.

—*André Gide*

There are no mistakes, no coincidences. All events are blessings given to us to learn from.

—*Elisabeth Kübler-Ross*

The art of life is not controlling what happens to us, but using what happens to us.

—*Gloria Steinem*

How wonderful it is that nobody need wait a single moment
before starting to improve the world.

—*Anne Frank*

•◆•

You don't get to choose how you're going to die. Or when.
You can only decide how you're going to live. Now.

—*Joan Baez*

•◆•

You shouldn't necessarily feel that your next step is the most
important one you'll ever take. It's not. You will go down many
paths that go nowhere.

—*Anderson Cooper*

•◆•

We must be willing to get rid of the life we've planned, so as to
have the life that is waiting for us.

—*Joseph Campbell*

•◆•

We are here and it is now. Further than that all human
knowledge is moonshine.

—*H. L. Mencken*

•◆•

There is more to life than increasing its speed.

—*Mahatma Gandhi*

Each day means a new twenty-four hours. Each day means everything's possible again. You live in the moment, you die in the moment, you take it all one day at a time.

—*Marie Lu*

Time is like a river of fleeting events, and its current is strong; as soon as something comes into sight, it is swept past us, and something else takes its place, and that too will be swept away.

—*Marcus Aurelius*

This is the real secret of life—to be completely engaged with what you are doing in the here and now. And instead of calling it work, realize it is play.

—*Alan Watts*

No matter what looms ahead, if you can eat today, enjoy the sunlight today, mix good cheer with friends today, enjoy it and bless God for it. Do not look back on happiness—or dream of it in the future. You are only sure of today; do not let yourself be cheated out of it.

—*Henry Ward Beecher*

For the meaning of life differs from man to man, from day to day and from hour to hour. What matters, therefore, is not the meaning of life in general but rather the specific meaning of a person's life at a given moment.

—*Viktor E. Frankl*

Live, travel, adventure, bless, and don't be sorry.

—*Jack Kerouac*

•-•-•

I exhort you also to take part in the great combat, which is the combat of life, and greater than every other earthly conflict.

—*Plato*

•-•-•

On the day that you were born, you began to die. Do not waste a single moment more!

—*Dilgo Khyentse Rinpoche*

•-•-•

Your time is limited, so don't waste it living someone else's life. Don't be trapped by dogma—which is living with the results of other people's thinking. Don't let the noise of others' opinions drown out your own inner voice. And most importantly, have the courage to follow your heart and intuition. They somehow already know what you truly want to become. Everything else is secondary.

—*Steve Jobs*

•-•-•

The journey of a thousand miles begins with one step.

—*Lao Tzu*

•-•-•

Go forth and set the world on fire.

—*St. Ignatius of Loyola*

Live as if you were living a second time, and as though you had acted wrongly the first time.

—Viktor E. Frankl

Radiate boundless love towards the entire world—above, below, and across—unhindered, without ill will, without enmity.

—Buddha

Live as if you were to die tomorrow. Learn as if you were to live forever.

—Mahatma Gandhi

Let us develop respect for all living things. Let us try to replace violence and intolerance with understanding and compassion. And love.

—Jane Goodall

Contributors

John Quincy Adams *(1767–1848)*—American statesman and sixth President of the United States

Joseph Addison *(1672–1719)*—English writer and politician

Mitch Albom *(b. 1958)*—American writer, journalist, screenwriter, and musician

Muhammad Ali *(1942–2016)*—American professional boxer, humanitarian, and philanthropist

St. Ambrose *(c. 340–397)*—German bishop and Doctor of the Church

Maya Angelou *(1928–2014)*—American writer and poet

St. Anthony of Padua *(1195–1231)*—Portuguese Franciscan preacher and reformer, Doctor of the Church

St. Thomas Aquinas *(c. 1225–74)*—Italian Dominican friar, priest, philosopher, theologian, and Doctor of the Church

Hannah Arendt *(1906–75)*—German-born American political philosopher

Aristotle *(384–322 B.C.)*—Greek philosopher

Guy Armstrong *(b. 19—)*—American teacher of meditation and leader of retreats

St. Augustine *(354–430)*—African-born bishop and Doctor of the Church

Marcus Aurelius *(121–180)*—Roman emperor and Stoic philosopher

Jane Austen *(1775–1817)*—English novelist

Sai Baba *(1835–1918)*—Indian spiritual master

Joan Baez *(b. 1941)*—American singer, songwriter, musician, and activist

Abdul Baha *('Abdu'l-Bahá) (1844–1921)*—Persian co-founder of the Bahá'í faith

James Baldwin *(1924–87)*—American writer and social critic

James Baraz *(b. 19—)*—American writer and teacher of mindfulness and meditation

Charlotte Joko Beck *(1917–2011)*—American Zen teacher and writer

Henry Ward Beecher *(1813–87)*—American clergyman and social reformer

Yehuda Berg *(b. 1972)*—Israeli writer

St. Bernard of Clairvaux *(1090–1153)*—French abbot and reformer

Ralph H. Blum *(b. 1932)*—American writer and cultural anthropologist

Jean Shinoda Bolen *(b. 1936)*—American psychiatrist and writer

Sylvia Boorstein *(b. 1936)*—American psychotherapist, writer, and teacher of mindfulness and meditation

Sarah Ban Breathnach *(b. 1947)*—American writer

Kathleen A. Brehony *(b. 1949)*—American psychologist, psychotherapist, and writer

Judson Brewer *(b. 19—)*—American psychiatrist, addiction expert, academic, and writer

Mel Brooks *(b. 1926)*—American actor, comedian, filmmaker, composer, and songwriter

Elizabeth Barrett Browning *(1806–61)*—English poet

Pearl S. Buck *(1892–1973)*—American writer

Buddha *(c. 6th century B.C.)*—founder of Buddhism

Leo Buscaglia *(1924–98)*—American writer, motivational speaker, and academic

Joseph Campbell *(1904–87)*—American mythologist, writer, and lecturer

Albert Camus *(1913–60)*—French writer

Richard Carlson *(1961–2006)*—American writer, psychotherapist, and speaker

Thomas Carlyle *(1795–1881)*—Scottish historian and political philosopher

Rachel Carson *(1907–64)*—American marine biologist, conservationist, and writer

Jimmy Carter *(b. 1924)*—American humanitarian, statesman, and writer; 39th President of the United States

George Washington Carver *(c. 1864–1943)*—American scientist, educator, and inventor

Willa Cather *(1873–1947)*—American novelist, poet, journalist, and editor

G. K. Chesterton *(1874–1936)*—English writer, philosopher, journalist, orator, and lay theologian

Pema Chödrön *(b. 1936)*—American-born Tibetan Buddhist nun and writer

Frederic Chopin *(1810–49)*—Polish pianist and composer

Deepak Chopra *(b. 1947)*—Indian-American physician, writer, and public speaker

Agatha Christie *(1890–1976)*—English crime novelist, short story writer, and playwright

Cicero *(106–43 B.C.)*—Roman statesman, orator, and writer

Paulo Coelho *(b. 1947)*—Brazilian novelist

Samuel Taylor Coleridge *(1772–1834)*—English poet, critic, and philosopher

Confucius *(551–479 B.C.)*—Chinese philosopher

Anderson Cooper *(b. 1967)*—American journalist and author

e.e. cummings *(1894–1962)*—American poet, painter, essayist, and playwright

Marie Curie *(1867–1934)*—Polish-French physicist and chemist

Dalai Lama *(Tenzin Gyatso) (b. 1935)*—Tibetan monk and religious leader

Charles Darwin *(1809–82)*—English naturalist and geologist

Ram Dass *(b. 1931)*—American spiritual teacher and writer

Deborah Day *(b. 19—)*—American writer and mental health counselor

Dorothy Day *(1897–1980)*—American journalist and activist

Simone de Beauvoir *(1908–86)*—French writer, philosopher, and activist

Ellen DeGeneres *(b. 1958)*—American comedian, television host, actress, writer, and producer

Charles Dickens *(1812–70)*—English novelist

Emily Dickinson *(1830–86)*—American poet

Annie Dillard *(b. 1945)*—American writer and academic

Isak Dinesen *(1885–1962)*—Danish writer

John Donne *(1572–1631)*—English poet and cleric

Margaret Drabble *(b. 1939)*—English writer and critic

Alexandre Dumas *(1802–70)*—French novelist and playwright

Wayne Dyer *(1940–2015)*—American writer, philosopher, and speaker

Amelia Earhart *(1897–1937 [presumed])*—American aviator and writer

Meister Eckhart *(1260–1328)*—German theologian, mystic, and philosopher

Max Ehrmann *(1872–1945)*—American writer, poet, and attorney

Albert Einstein *(1879–1955)*—German-born American physicist

Duane Elgin *(b. 1943)*—American writer, educator, speaker, and activist

George Eliot *(1819–80)*—English novelist

T. S. Eliot *(1888–1965)*—American-born British publisher, poet, and essayist

Ralph Waldo Emerson *(1803–82)*—American essayist and poet

Epictetus *(c. 55–135)*—Greek Stoic philosopher

Epicurus *(341–270 B.C.)*—Greek philosopher

Erasmus *(c. 1466–1536)*—Dutch Roman Catholic priest, humanist, social critic, teacher, and theologian

Louise Erdrich *(b. 1954)*—Chippewa-American novelist and poet

Euripides *(480–406 B.C.)*—Greek playwright

William Faulkner *(1897–1962)*—American writer

Norman Fischer *(b. 1946)*—Jewish-American Soto Zen roshi, poet, and Buddhist writer

Theodor Fontane *(1819–98)*—German novelist and poet

Anatole France *(1844–1924)*—French poet, novelist, and journalist

Pope Francis *(b. 1936)*—266th pope of the Roman Catholic Church

St. Francis de Sales *(1567–1622)*—French bishop, missionary, and Doctor of the Church

St. Francis of Assisi *(c. 1182–1226)*—Italian preacher, mystic, and founder of the Order of Friars Minor (Franciscans)

Anne Frank *(1929–45)*—German-born diarist

Viktor E. Frankl *(1905–97)*—Austrian-born neurologist and psychiatrist

Benjamin Franklin *(1706–90)*—American statesman and philosopher

David Frost *(1939–2013)*—English journalist, writer, comedian, and television host

Margaret Fuller *(1810–50)*—American journalist, critic, and women's rights activist

Indira Gandhi *(1917–84)*—Indian politician and Prime Minister of India

Mahatma Gandhi *(1869–1948)*—Indian nationalist leader

Shakti Gawain *(b. 1948)*—American New Age writer

Richard Gere *(b. 1949)*—American actor, humanitarian, and activist

Christopher Germer *(b. 19—)*—American clinical psychologist and writer

A. Bartlett Giamatti *(1938–89)*—American academic and seventh Commissioner of Major League Baseball

Kahlil Gibran *(1883–1931)*—Lebanese-American mystical poet and philosopher

André Gide *(1869–1951)*—French writer

Charlotte Perkins Gilman *(1860–1935)*—American activist, sociologist, lecturer, and writer

Goethe *(Johann Wolfgang von) (1749–1832)*—German poet and dramatist

Oliver Goldsmith *(1728–74)*—Irish novelist, playwright, and poet

Elisha Goldstein *(b. 19—)*—American psychologist, educator, speaker, and writer

Daniel Goleman *(b. 1946)*—American writer, psychologist, and journalist

Jane Goodall *(b. 1934)*—English primatologist, ethologist, anthropologist, and activist

Martha Graham *(1894–1991)*—American dancer and choreographer

Germaine Greer *(b. 1939)*—Australian writer and activist

Hafiz of Shiraz *(Hafez) (b. 1326)*—Persian poet

Alex Haley *(1921–92)*—American writer

Thich Nhat Hanh *(b. 1926)*—Vietnamese Buddhist monk, Zen master, poet, and peace activist

Goldie Hawn *(b. 1945)*—American actress and director

Father Edward Hays *(1931–2016)*—American Roman Catholic priest and writer

Ernest Hemingway *(1899–1961)*—American writer

Heraclitus *(c. 535–475 B.C.)*—Greek philosopher

Rabbi Abraham Joshua Heschel *(1907–1972)*—Polish-born American rabbi, theologian, and philosopher

Hans Hofmann *(1880–1966)*—German-born American painter

Horace *(65–8 B.C.)*—Roman poet and satirist

Victor Hugo *(1802–85)*—French poet, novelist, and dramatist

Aldous Huxley *(1894–1963)*—English writer and philosopher

St. Ignatius of Loyola *(1491–1556)*—Spanish priest, spiritual writer, and founder of the Society of Jesus (Jesuits)

Washington Irving *(1783–1859)*—American writer, historian, and diplomat

William James *(1842–1910)*—American philosopher and psychologist

Thomas Jefferson *(1743–1826)*—American Founding Father and third President of the United States

Steve Jobs *(1955–2011)*—American entrepreneur and inventor

St. John Paul II *(1920–2005)*—264th pope of the Roman Catholic Church; canonized in April 2014

Samuel Johnson *(1709–84)*—English writer

Joseph Joubert *(1754–1824)*—French moralist and essayist

Carl Jung *(1875–1961)*—Swiss psychiatrist and psychotherapist

Jon Kabat-Zinn *(b. 1944)*—American academic, writer, and creator of the Stress Reduction Clinic and the Center for Mindfulness in Medicine, Health Care, and Society at the University of Massachusetts Medical School

Father Thomas Keating *(b. 1923)*—American Trappist monk, priest, writer, and architect in the development of Centering Prayer

Helen Keller *(1880–1968)*—American writer, activist, and educator

Thomas à Kempis *(1380–1471)*—Dutch priest, monk, and writer

Jack Kerouac *(1922–69)*—American novelist, poet, and student of Buddhism

Sue Monk Kidd *(b. 1948)*—American writer

Søren Kierkegaard *(1813–55)*—Danish philosopher, theologian, poet, social critic, and writer

Martin Luther King Jr. *(1929–68)*—American clergyman and civil rights leader

Jack Kornfield *(b. 1945)*—American meditation teacher, writer, and founder and director of Spirit Rock Center

Jiddu Krishnamurti *(1895–1986)*—Indian writer and speaker

Elisabeth Kübler-Ross *(1926–2004)*—Swiss-American psychiatrist and writer

Rabbi Harold Kushner *(b. 1935)*—American rabbi and writer

Madeleine L'Engle *(1918–2007)*—American writer

Anne Lamott *(b. 1954)*—American novelist and nonfiction writer

Abraham Lincoln *(1809–65)*—American statesman and 16th President of the United States

Anne Morrow Lindbergh *(1906–2001)*—American writer

John Locke *(1632–1704)*—English philosopher

Allan Lokos *(b. 19—)*—American teacher of meditation, writer, and founder of Community Meditation Center

Audre Lorde *(1934–92)*—American writer, feminist, and activist

James Russell Lowell *(1819–91)*—American poet, critic, editor, and diplomat

Marie Lu *(b. 1984)*—Chinese-born American young adult writer

Martin Luther *(1483–1546)*—German Reformation leader

Rachel Maddow *(b. 1973)*—American political commentator and writer

Nelson Mandela *(1918–2013)*—South African political leader, activist, humanitarian, philanthropist, and lawyer

Bob Marley *(1945–81)*—Jamaican musician and activist

Harriet Martineau *(1802–76)*—English writer and journalist

Henri Matisse *(1869–1954)*—French artist

Kathleen McDonald *(b. 19—)*—American-born Tibetan nun, writer, and teacher of Buddhism and meditation

Margaret Mead *(1901–78)*—American cultural anthropologist and writer

H. L. Mencken *(1880–1956)*—German-American writer, critic, and satirist

Thomas Merton *(1915–68)*—American religious writer and mystic

Henry Miller *(1891–1980)*—American writer

A. A. Milne *(1882–1956)*—English writer

Kenji Miyazawa *(1896–1933)*—Japanese poet and children's author

Montaigne *(Michel de) (1533–92)*—French essayist

Susan Moon *(b. 19—)*—American writer, editor, and meditation teacher

Henry Moore *(1898–1986)*—Anglo-Irish sculptor and artist

St. Thomas More *(1478–1535)*—English lawyer, philosopher, humanist, and writer

William Morris *(1834–96)*—English designer, poet, novelist, and activist

Robert Moses *(1888–1981)*—American city planner

John Muir *(1838–1914)*—Scottish-born American naturalist

Robert Muller *(1923–2010)*—American global education advocate and former Assistant Secretary-General of the United Nations

Alice Munro *(b. 1931)*—Canadian writer

Haruki Murakami *(b. 1949)*—Japanese writer

Friedrich Nietzsche *(1844–1900)*—German philosopher, cultural critic, poet, and scholar

Anaïs Nin *(1903–77)*—French-born American writer

Henri Nouwen *(1932–96)*—Dutch religious writer and theologian

Joyce Carol Oates *(b. 1938)*—American writer

Barack Obama *(b. 1961)*—American politician and 44th President of the United States

Michelle Obama *(b. 1961)*—American lawyer, writer, activist, and First Lady of the United States

Mary Oliver *(b. 1935)*—American poet

James Oppenheim *(1882–1932)*—American poet and social worker

Osho *(1931–90)*—Indian mystic, guru, and spiritual teacher

Ovid *(43 B.C.–17 A.D.)*—Roman poet

Cynthia Ozick *(b. 1928)*—American writer

Sara Paddison *(b. 19—)*—Writer

Dolly Parton *(b. 1946)*—American singer-songwriter, actress, writer, and humanitarian

Blaise Pascal *(1623–62)*—French mathematician, physicist, and religious philosopher

Alan Paton *(1903–88)*—South African writer and activist

M. Scott Peck *(1936–2005)*—American psychiatrist and writer

Albert Pike *(1809–91)*—American attorney, soldier, and writer

Steven Pinker *(b. 1954)*—Canadian-born American cognitive scientist, psychologist, linguist, professor, and writer

Plato *(c. 428–348 B.C.)*—Greek philosopher and writer

Plutarch *(c. 46–122)*—Greek philosopher and writer

Li Po *(Li Bai) (701–762)*—Chinese poet

Alexander Pope *(1688–1744)*—English poet

Hugh Prather *(1938–2010)*—American writer, lay minister, and counselor

Marcel Proust *(1871–1922)*—French novelist, essayist, and critic

Anna Quindlen *(b. 1953)*—American novelist and journalist

Mary Anne Radmacher *(b. 19—)*—American writer and artist

Amit Ray *(b. 1960)*—Indian author and spiritual master

Christopher Reeve *(1952–2004)*—American actor, director, producer, and activist

Matthieu Ricard *(b. 1946)*—French-born writer, Buddhist monk, and humanitarian

Rainer Maria Rilke *(1875–1926)*—Bohemian-Austrian poet and novelist

Dilgo Khyentse Rinpoche *(1910–91)*—Tibetan-born scholar, poet, meditation master, and principal holder of the Nyingma lineage

Sogyal Rinpoche *(b. 1947)*—Tibetan Dzogchen lama of the Nyingma tradition, spiritual director, and writer

Theodore Roosevelt *(1858–1919)*—American statesman, reformer, and naturalist; 26th President of the United States

St. Rose of Lima *(1586–1617)*—Peruvian lay member of Dominican order

Jean-Jacques Rousseau *(1712–78)*—Swiss-born French philosopher, writer, and composer

J. K. Rowling *(b. 1965)*—English novelist, screenwriter, and film producer

Rumi *(1207–1273)*—Persian poet, jurist, scholar, theologian, and Sufi mystic

John Ruskin *(1819–1900)*—English art critic, artist, and philanthropist

Sharon Salzberg *(b. 1952)*—American writer and teacher of Buddhism

George Sand *(1804–76)*—French novelist and memoirist

George Santayana *(1863–1952)*—Spanish-American poet and philosopher

Esmeralda Santiago *(b. 1948)*—Puerto Rican writer

William Saroyan *(1908–81)*—American writer and dramatist

Jean-Paul Sartre *(1905–80)*—French philosopher, writer, and activist

Remez Sasson *(b. 19—)*—American writer and founder of SuccessConsciousness.com

Albert Schweitzer *(1875–1965)*—French-German theologian, journalist, scholar, missionary, and physician

Julian Seifter *(b. 19—)*—American nephrologist and writer

Seneca *(c. 4 B.C.–65 A.D.)*—Roman philosopher, statesman, and dramatist

George Bernard Shaw *(1856–1950)*—Irish dramatist and critic

Gail Sheehy *(b. 1937)*—American writer, journalist, and speaker

Maria Shriver *(b. 1955)*—American journalist, writer, and activist

Daniel J. Siegel *(b. 1957)*—American physician, academic, and executive director of Mindsight Institute

Russell Simmons *(b. 1957)*—American entrepreneur, producer, and writer

Betty Smith *(1896–1972)*—American novelist

Patti Smith *(b. 1946)*—American singer-songwriter, poet, and artist

Socrates *(c. 470–399 B.C.)*—Greek philosopher

Sophocles *(d. 406 B.C.)*—Greek playwright

Muriel Spark *(1918–2006)*—Scottish novelist

Luther Standing Bear *(1868–1939)*—Oglala Lakota American writer, educator, philosopher, and actor

Publius Statius *(45–96)*—Roman poet

Gertrude Stein *(1874–1946)*—American avant-garde writer

Gloria Steinem *(b. 1936)*—American writer, journalist, and political and social activist

Robert Louis Stevenson *(1850–94)*—Scottish novelist, poet, and essayist

Alexandra Stoddard *(b. 1941)*—American writer, interior designer, and lifestyle philosopher

Harriet Beecher Stowe *(1811–96)*—American writer and abolitionist

Jill Bolte Taylor *(b. 1959)*—American neuroanatomist, writer, and public speaker

Edwin Way Teale *(1899–1980)*—American naturalist, photographer, and writer

Sara Teasdale *(1884–1933)*—American poet

Pierre Teilhard de Chardin *(1881–1955)*—French Jesuit priest, philosopher, paleontologist, and geologist

Corrie ten Boom *(1892–1983)*—Dutch activist and writer

Terence *(c. 190–159 B.C.)*—Roman playwright

St. Teresa of Avila *(1515–82)*—Spanish mystic, Carmelite nun, reformer, Doctor of the Church

Mother Teresa *(1910–97)*—Albanian-born Roman Catholic nun and missionary; beatified in 2003 and canonized in September 2016

William Makepeace Thackeray *(1811–63)*—English novelist, poet, and satirist

St. Thérèse of Lisieux *(1873–97)*—French Carmelite mystic and Doctor of the Church

Henry David Thoreau *(1817–62)*—American philosopher, writer, and naturalist

Elizabeth Thornton *(Mary Forrest George) (1940–2010)*—English-Canadian novelist

Howard Thurman *(1899–1981)*—American writer, philosopher, educator, and civil rights leader

Paul Tillich *(1886–1965)*—German-American Christian existentialist philosopher and Lutheran theologian

Alvin Toffler *(1928–2016)*—American writer and futurist

Eckhart Tolle *(b. 1948)*—German-born spiritual teacher and writer

Renee Peterson Trudeau *(b. 1966)*—American writer, life coach, and speaker

Desmond Tutu *(b. 1931)*—South African social rights activist and retired Anglican bishop

Mark Twain *(1835–1910)*—American writer and humorist

Chuang Tzu *(Zhuang Zhou) (c. 370–287 B.C.)*—Chinese philosopher

Lao Tzu *(Laozi) (c. 6th century B.C.)*—Chinese poet and philosopher

John Updike *(1932–2009)*—American writer and critic

Henry Van Dyke *(1852–1933)*—American writer, educator, and clergyman

Voltaire *(1694–1778)*—French philosopher and writer

Alice Walker *(b. 1944)*—American novelist, poet, and activist

Charles Dudley Warner *(1829–1900)*—American essayist and novelist

Alan Watts *(1915–73)*—English philosopher, writer, and speaker

Simone Weil *(1909–43)*—French philosopher, mystic, and activist

Paul Dudley White *(1886–1973)*—American physician

Alfred North Whitehead *(1861–1947)*—English mathematician and philosopher

Walt Whitman *(1819–92)*—American poet, essayist, and journalist

Elie Wiesel *(1928–2016)*—Romanian-born American writer, professor, political activist, and humanitarian

Marianne Williamson *(b. 1952)*—American spiritual teacher, writer, and lecturer

Oprah Winfrey *(b. 1954)*—American media mogul, actress, and philanthropist

Virginia Woolf *(1882–1941)*—English writer

William Wordsworth *(1770–1850)*—English poet

William Butler Yeats *(1865–1939)*—Irish poet

Lin Yutang *(1895–1976)*—Chinese writer and inventor